AN ESSAY ON THE
RESTORATION OF PROPERTY

To the parents of the Directors.

AN ESSAY ON THE
RESTORATION
OF
PROPERTY

BY

HILAIRE BELLOC

With a New Introduction by John Sharpe,
and the IHS Press Introduction of the 2002 edition

Norfolk, VA
2009

ISBN-13: 978-1-60570-025-0
ISBN-10: 1-60570-025-8

Library of Congress Cataloging-in-Publication Data

Belloc, Hilaire, 1870-1953.
An essay on the restoration of property / by Hilaire
Belloc.
      p. cm.
   ISBN-13: 978-1-60570-025-0 (alk. paper)
   1. Land reform--England. 2. Land tenure--England. 3.
Property--England. I. Title
      HD1333.G72 E543 2009
      333.3'142--dc21
                  2002073663

Printed in the United States of America.

This edition has largely preserved the spelling, punctuation, and formatting of Belloc's original 1936 edition. Editors' notes will be found at the end of the text, while original notes by the author are included as footnotes.

FRONTISPIECE: Haytime in the Cotswolds by James Bateman.

IHS Press is the only publisher dedicated exclusively
to the Social Teachings of the Catholic Church.

Contents

PAGE

Introduction to the
Second IHS Press Edition vii
John Sharpe

Introduction to the
First IHS Press Edition xi
The Directors, IHS Press

Preface xxiii
Hilaire Belloc

AN ESSAY ON THE RESTORATION
OF PROPERTY I

Notes 83

"...though certainly it is impossible to change a false philosophy in time to save the situation, yet there may be enough normal love of freedom remaining, however feeble, to be used as a starting point. There may be embers aglow here and there, sufficient to start the small beginnings of a flame."

Introduction to the
Second IHS Press Edition

EVERAL YEARS AGO I HAD THE PLEASURE AND
privilege of participating in the publication of
the first new edition of Belloc's *Essay on the Restoration of Property* to come out in several decades.
At the time (and as the original introduction indicates), we
had lamented the burgeoning U.S. national debt, the atrocious
average personal savings rate, the effectively empty leger on the
"asset" side of American corporate books, and the all-too-well-
known state of the modern home "owner," who *rents* his home
to the tune of a 30-year compound interest "favor" provided by
the decidedly non-local mortgage bank. This, of course, is all
notwithstanding the real evil that has plagued Western economic life for over a century–namely the general and social
separation of labor from capital and the proletarianization of
the average man and family that such a separation implies.

No one expected things to get better immediately–in fact
the expectation was at the time that things would probably
get worse before any trend in the opposite direction ensued.
As Belloc has elsewhere written, "Things will not get right
again . . . until society becomes as simple as it used be, and
we shall have to go through a pretty bad time before we get
back to that."* But it certainly would have strained even my
(admittedly naïve) credulity to have thought then that just

---

* *Economics for Helen* (Norfolk, Va.: IHS Press, 2004 [1924]), p. 163.

eight years later, the U.S. public debt would be approaching $13 trillion – more than ten percent of which would have been incurred from expenditure upon two unprovoked and illegal wars; the country would be spending $388 billion on a cold-war era attack aircraft for the purpose of hunting down allegedly "terrorist" nomads in southwest Asian caves; and that the American budget deficit (a.k.a. the annual debt increase) would be projected at close to $1 trillion for every year of the next decade. And this, of course, leaves aside the "financial crisis" of the last two years (memorably described by William Pfaff as perpetrated by "mortgage scam operators, real estate salesmen and brokers, and debt repackagers in the great globalized free market, who in recent years managed to turn home mortgage rip-offs to the poor in America into an international crisis unforeseen by either the former financial masters of the universe or the world's central bankers"*) – that everyone seems to be talking about, but few seem genuinely to understand. Fewer still see the irony in speaking of a "crisis" – as if before 2008 economic affairs were sound, healthy, and in perfect harmony with the natural moral law!

In any event, what all of the foregoing can only mean is that token wealth, as Fr. McNabb so presciently termed modern money, has lost every last shred of its connection with anything of real value. Bailouts, debt swaps, and even mortgages are simply the deadly fictions of a social system that has been erected upon the smug, belligerent, and violent denial of reality itself. At the back of this sorry state of affairs, economically speaking, are two simple root causes, upon which Belloc put his finger precisely in his 1936 essay. One "cause of the evil," he says, "would appear to be unchecked competition" (p. 31 of the present edition). That this is so is obvious from many more methods of measurement and lines of inquiry than the space at my disposition permits me to mention. Even

---

*"International Finance Pillaging Poor Nations," March 2, 2010, http://www.williampfaff.com/modules/news/article.php?storyid=454.

professional historians attempting to survey the rise of capitalism in the early national period of the American Republic pay unintentional homage to this idea: that capitalism – which some of them still not surprisingly struggle to define – cannot really have taken root in this country until certain customary and legal limits upon public or commercial economic activity became inoperative, thus leaving the playing field open for the practical workings of *laissez faire*.* Also implied by this recent historical work, along with common sense and Belloc's explicit claim, is that the transition from a traditional economic order to one which, in the name of capitalism, actually denies to the mass of men and families the ownership of genuinely productive property was produced by, "ultimate[ly,] . . . a certain mood – an attitude of mind" – an attitude frankly opposed to "a public opinion supporting well-divided property, [and to one] which takes well-divided property for granted." It is to this mood or attitude that Mike Merrill refers in noting that

> [i]n the antebellum era, most Americans were not interested in encouraging the unlimited accumulation of private fortunes, or in expanding the most dependent forms of wage labor, or in increasing the financial opportunities available to the wealthy, or in commodifying everything. But they did want to protect the relatively widespread distribution of private property, to ensure that wage labor could continue to serve as a stepping stone to independent proprietorship, and to increase the financial opportunities available to the many. They also wanted to preserve,

---

*The work of Gordon Wood and Michael Merrill is most illustrative in this regard, though our sympathy with the latter's view to the exclusion of the former is perhaps too obvious to require much discussion. See, e.g., Michael Merrill, "The Anticapitalist Origins of the United States," *Review* 13, no. 4 (Fall 1990): 465-97 and "Putting 'Capitalism' in Its Place: A Review of Recent Literature," *The William and Mary Quarterly* 52, no. 2 (Apr 1995): 315-26; and Gordon S. Wood, "The Enemy Is Us: Democratic Capitalism in the Early Republic," *Journal of the Early Republic* 16, no. 2 (Summer 1996): 293-308 and "Was America Born Capitalist," *The Wilson Quarterly* 23, no. 2 (Spring 1999): 36-46.

as a hedge against the vagaries of the market, broad access to goods and resources through noncommercial forms of exchange such as barter and inheritance.*

In response to the collapse of institutional safeguards for the wide distribution of productive property represented by the guilds in Europe and similar laws and customs in the antebellum United States, the most obvious remedial course, if at the same time (and on one level) the most difficult, will be for an individual man or his family to reunite what capitalism separated and socialism seeks to sunder permanently, namely, labor and capital, through the ownership of a productive piece of property, whether in land or in the tools and know-how of a craft or trade. At the same time, it is the common, communal effort, even on a small scale, that will most likely be the forum in which the customs and attitudes Merrill details may be restored—and to which therefore the men and families who have the time, talent, and disposition should devote themselves.

It is in service of one component of this effort—the unabashed attempt to facilitate a genuine ideological revolution undermining the ethos of industrial capitalism—that IHS Press intends to continue its modest but, *Deo volente*, salutary work. At the same time, as suggested by Belloc's reminder—"considering how a fortress may be attacked with the means at [our] disposal, it is [our] first business to ask . . . where its weak points are to be found" (33)—the most likely field of immediate victory is not the ideological one. Rather, as Belloc details in what follows, there are "things that can be done even now . . . with some chance of partial and limited success" (34)—and it is these things that men of action and good will must begin, and begin at once.

> John Sharpe
> The Epiphany of Our Lord Jesus Christ
> January 6, 2010

---

*Merrill, "Putting 'Capitalism' in Its Place," 322–23.

Introduction to the
First IHS Press Edition

People do not live and work in order to buy stocks.

—*The Nation*
August 19, 2002

NSOFAR AS HILAIRE BELLOC IS KNOWN AT ALL BY the modern world, he is known only as a writer of children's tales. He is known in his most innocuous and least-threatening aspect – an easy escape for those who do not wish to have comfortable lives and convenient assumptions challenged and exposed. Yet even a fair appreciation of Belloc's stories for children is, if taken in isolation, ultimately a failed appreciation of Belloc himself; to appreciate this fierce critic of modernity as merely a children's writer is not really to *appreciate* Belloc at all. It is to appreciate an *aspect* of him, much the way he accused non-Catholic historians of appreciating this or that aspect of European history. Only those who can truly sympathize with a life of crusading for the Truth can fully appreciate Belloc's career, for Belloc crusaded for Truth in all fields, at all times, and in every subject: in fiction, in religion, in politics, and in economics.

Yes, economics.

Modern practitioners of the "dismal science" would be reluctant, of course, to grant Belloc any status as an "economist;" nor would Belloc have wanted such a status. For modern economists spring from a tradition both foreign and hostile to that which nurtured Belloc. Theirs is a tradition of materialist philosophy and an obsession with a mere technical analysis of what is; today the analysis is more often than not an attempted explanation of what *isn't* (like corporate assets or the value of a portfolio of futures commodities). Belloc's is rather a science of reality, based upon a conception not merely of what is, in this vale of tears, but more importantly of what ought to be, according to Divine and natural law.

Readers therefore will not find, in Belloc's works, traces of that skepticism which speaks of politics as merely the "art of the possible," and of economics as a science of hypotheses based solely on observable phenomena and codified into a collection of equations, charts and graphs. As an integral Catholic, Belloc followed in the footsteps of St. Thomas the *realist*, who spoke of Politics as the moral science "which considers the proper ordering of men," and Political Economy as that science "concerned with the using of money...for the good estate of the home."

Thus is Belloc's treatment of economic questions, in *Restoration of Property*, *Economics for Helen*, and the *Servile State*, concerned with *reality* in both its profoundest sense and its most practical. *Profound* because Belloc has always before him a knowledge of the Purpose of the sciences, a knowledge that all of the tools, techniques, and means employed by them are given clear and well-defined directions and orientations by their various Purposes. And *practical* because when Belloc considers economic matters he is concerned not with the pie (-in-the-sky) charts of modern economic theoreticians, but rather with how to solve the problem of securing for men the material necessities of life in a manner most befitting both their dignity as free men and their sublimity as souls destined for Heaven. There is nothing novel in so doing; Belloc simply follows St. Thomas in subordinating the acquisition of wealth to the true needs of man: "That a man may lead a good life, two things are required. The chief requisite is virtuous action.... The other requisite, which is secondary and quasi-instrumental in character, is a sufficiency of material goods, the use of which is necessary for virtuous action" (*On Kingship*, I, xv).

Such an approach has for a long time seemed quaint and "unrealistic" to a society concerned with satisfying "the bottom line" and getting "more bang for the buck." Has seemed quaint – until recently.

Today such an approach is touted almost as a "revelation" by many moderns who, all of a sudden, are realizing – even if unconsciously – that St. Thomas had the order of economic priorities *exactly right*. Protesting the domination of economic activity by finance, and the lawlessness of corporate America, a recent editorial in the *Nation* declares, "The larger purpose of the economic order, including Wall Street, is to support the material conditions for human existence." How charmingly similar to the approach taken by the classical and Catholic political economists, men forming a constant and coherent tradition extending over 2200 years, from Aristotle of the fourth century B.C. to Charles Devas of the early 20ᵗʰ century A.D.!

The editorial continues:

> During the past two decades, a profound inversion has occurred in the governing values of US economic life and, in turn, captured politics and elite discourse – the triumph of finance over the real economy. In the natural order of capitalism, the financial system is supposed to serve the economy of production – goods and services, jobs and incomes – but the narrow values of Wall Street have become the master.

Such an observation is both a step forward and a step back. A step forward, because it confirms that there are some who have managed to keep a strong enough hold on common sense to recognize that, ultimately, all of the financial wizardry in the world means nothing if it doesn't translate into a secure provisioning of the average family with the goods and services that are necessary for a healthy and becoming life.

A step backward, though, because to demand that the "natural order of capitalism" subject finance to real economic values is to ask of it something that it was never intended to provide. A system based purely on free competition cannot possibly be expected to produce, of its own nature, the subordination of finance and capital to the needs of men, precisely because those "little" needs do not possess the economic might that would allow them to compete successfully with huge conglomerations of business and money. "It's a jungle out there" is no quaint reference to a family trip to the zoo; the cliché only too well describes modern economic life as it is practiced and accepted by modern men in the "civilized" West. "Survival of the fittest" does not produce order, harmony, and well-distributed bliss when the operative principle is not an "indifferent" and inanimate Mother Nature, but rather the capacity of fallen Man to desire an infinite amount of wealth, regardless of the consequences for himself or his neighbor.

No matter how obvious such an observation might seem, even the most brilliant of modern economists remain shocked and surprised that a system which does not have any built-in restraint upon man's avarice can produce such devastating results: "I can only say," said John K. Galbraith in a recent interview with the U.K.-based *Independent*, "I hadn't expected to see this problem on anything like the magnitude of the last few months – the separation of ownership from management, the monopolization of control by irresponsible personal money-makers."

One wonders what exactly Mr. Galbraith had expected to see. Such "shock and surprise" can only be attributed to a failure – intentional or otherwise – to look not at the figures but at the facts; facts of both history and logic, which reveal that the glory of the Christian West consisted not "in every man doing what he pleases," as the great Leo XIII put it in his magnificent encyclical *Libertas*, "for this would simply end in turmoil and confusion;" but rather in submission, both individual *and social*, to the Eternal Law, a Law that remains even today written on the hearts of men, and which was at one time written also in their constitutions, statutes, codes, and charters.

"He that hath ears to hear, let him hear" (St. Matthew xi:1), Our Lord said. Few, even among Catholics, did hear. In retrospect the Church's prescience is striking:

> ...it is obvious that not only is wealth concentrated in our times but an immense power and despotic economic dictatorship is consolidated in the hands of a few, who often are not owners but only the trustees and managing directors of invested funds which they administer according to their own arbitrary will and pleasure.

This isn't a recent CNN financial "special report;" this is Pope Pius XI in *Quadragesimo Anno* over seventy years ago. Men will learn eventually, and if they insist on rejecting the received wisdom of generations past, they do not thereby succeed at invalidating it; they merely condemn themselves to learning it, time and again, by ever grimmer experience.

***

THUS IS THE time more propitious now than it has been in recent memory to re-introduce the wisdom of the Distributists – those such as Fr. Vincent McNabb, G.K. Chesterton, Arthur Penty, and others, including, of course, Hilaire Belloc, who sought consistently, coherently, and unapologetically, to apply the Social Doctrine of the Church to 20th-century problems. Modern men seem to be in a rare, though doubtless brief, mood of willingness – and almost eagerness – to think about all things economic. We avail ourselves, therefore, of the opportunity herewith to put before the reader Belloc's classic *Essay on the Restoration of Property*.

That the *Essay* does not include comprehensive figures and statistics typical of studies of the vast fabric of economic life should be obvious from its short length; that will be, no doubt, welcome news to most. Though it may not be so to some who might be tempted to ask, "What else is there to discuss in the field of economics?" Such a question stems from the fact that there are few today who have any exposure to a method of reasoning which "begins at the beginning," as Belloc says in his famous essay on Industrial Capitalism. It is a method which starts with the Purpose of economic life, as wise men have always conceived of it, and as even those not so wise have recently and reluctantly admitted. It examines that purpose, and proceeds to propose means which are fitted to achieving it. It deals with facts – facts of human nature, facts of history, *hard* facts of economic life such as land, homes, clothing, tools, and trades. What it does not deal with is isolated bits of data which can be manipulated at will, and presented in a very pretty package, in order to reflect whatever degree of reality – or *unre*-ality – the situation requires.

What is, therefore, both assumed and implied by such a method is that man is the master of his destiny, and his mastery extends even to things economic. Man has free will, and the question at the root of Belloc's reasoning in *Restoration of Property* – like the reasoning of St. Thomas and all those who followed him – concerns how man should use that free will in order to achieve the end of economic life, namely, "the good estate of the home."

This question of freedom is central to the *Restoration*, both implicitly and explicitly.

Implicitly because the *Essay*, and the science of Political Economy in general, assumes that it is up to man to regulate, according to his free decisions, economic forces and economic activity in order to achieve the end desired. The political economist does *not* concede that there is an economic "law," inviolable and unchangeable, that must be obeyed the way man obeys the laws of an inanimate universe, in spite of the fact that some Catholics – interested perhaps in currying favor with rehabilitated liberals who worship the "free market" – themselves maintain that very position, based upon out-of-context quotations from Scholastic theologians who are speciously (and scandalously!) accused of laying the foundations of modern capitalism. Such a conception is foreign to the true economic science; it is a conception born of "the principles of rationalism" which produced, as Pius XI explained, a "body of economic teaching far removed from the true moral law." The true economic science deals with real men, who can make decisions, right or wrong, or leave them unmade; and thus the central question of economics as with politics is how *ought* things to be ordered. Belloc himself reminds us of this point in the *Essay*:

> The defenders of industrial capitalism – such few of them as are left – and those with the same type of mind who defend Socialism, and its only logical form, Communism, have told us over and over again that amalgamation is inevitable. They call it an "economic necessity" because they think that any instrument or method cheaper or more efficient for the special purpose of production or transport must necessarily oust the somewhat less cheap or somewhat less efficient. They also imply that there is a necessity for the greedier man and the more cunning man to eat up the more generous and less instructed.
>
> They who talk thus confuse what they here call "necessity" with that true necessity imposed by universal physical laws independent of the human will.

Belloc deals with the question of freedom explicitly as well: he examines how best to guarantee man's economic freedom. This freedom, for Belloc, is not the one imagined by the classical liberals and their Objectivist, libertarian, or "conservative" heirs. It is not a defense of license – man's freedom to do no matter what to no matter whom, and the silly conception that such a *capitalist* freedom is the only one which truly respects man's free nature. Belloc's is a defense of the economic freedom which comes from the possession of sufficient productive property, such that a man need not depend upon his employer for a wage, but has rather to depend upon himself and *his* land, craft, tools, and trade for his sustenance.

At first hearing, the notion is almost incomprehensible! Belloc himself recognized how difficult it would be for us moderns to understand: "When men have become wage slaves they think in terms of income. When they are economically free they think in terms of property." But think in such a fashion we must, if we are ever to remedy the current disordered state of affairs in which man's real needs are subordinated to the exigencies of the amassing of financial wealth.

For those who are still loath to admit it, a quick glance at the facts should put to rest any notion that the current system makes man as much an owner of real wealth and property as was his noble, European, yeoman ancestor, to whom Belloc and his colleagues so often refer.

(1) "Conservatives" like to speak of the culture of death; they would do well to focus their attention on the culture of *debt*, for the institutionalized Usury so characteristic of the post-medieval world is as deadly to society, and as unnatural and unproductive, as are the host of cultural ills ranging from abortion to homosexuality to euthanasia. Those who claim to be home-owners forget that in most cases the real homeowners are the banks, and that they themselves are on a rent-to-own program which normally lasts 30 years and sees a "modest" compound interest rate translate into a payment in real terms of *several times* the value of the home. Meanwhile, the culture of debt offers the opportunity to squander whatever ownership one has acquired by re-mortgaging a home in exchange for cash to be consumed on luxury items of all kinds. The whole of mortgage debt in the U.S. is close to five and a half trillion dollars; the rate of savings as a percent of disposable income has remained *near zero* for several years; and the ratio of household debt to disposable income is now over one hundred percent! So much for modern man, the proud "home owner."

(2) Today, finance, economics, and wealth itself is largely a fiction. Few own real, tangible property; most own and deal in electronic assets. A single day's change in the U.S. stock market of a few percent "creates" or "destroys" over a trillion dollars worth of "wealth," though such a change affects nothing in companies' physical assets, or in their ability to produce a prod-

uct or provide a service. Americans who have been forced, both by inflation and the going economic "advice," to put their hard-earned money into stocks have been afforded the opportunity to watch the elimination of billions of dollars worth of retirement funds and pension plans tied up in stocks and mutual funds as a result of corporate bankruptcies or stock market devaluations. And all of this takes place without a single tangible asset – without real wealth – ever changing hands.

Meanwhile, the "wealth and power" of the American corporation is sustained by a record $4.7 trillion worth of "credit," which must eventually be paid back to venture capitalists, banks, and bond-holders. Add to that the fact that corporate accounting seems ever more determined *not* to account for anything. A financial newsletter recently reminded its readers of just how false and deceptive corporate financial statements can be, through the use of "infamous *'pro forma* earnings' – a calculation designed to exclude as many expenses as possible from the reported earnings. Expert practitioners of the *pro forma* charade," the newsletter continued, "could paint a very pleasing picture of a company's financial health, no matter how grim the actual cash flow trend."

And the fictitious financial wheel is kept rolling by the "mother of all creditors," the U.S. Federal Reserve, a *private* banking corporation which, since its foundation in 1913, has held the reigns of financial power in America through its strangle-hold on credit, a power which Pius XI called the ability to "regulate the flow, so to speak, of the life-blood whereby the entire economic system lives" (*QA*, 106). Should any of the big investment firms find themselves exposed to excessive risk, thanks to their own financial irresponsibility, they will no doubt be labeled "too big to fail;" they can be kept alive by a creation of cash (out of thin air) by the private banking cartel which hasn't balked at floating even the U.S. government to the tune of a *$6.12 trillion public debt.*

(3) The financial wealth which does exist is concentrated, to an unprecedented degree, into a very few hands. That of the

top one percent of households in America exceeds the combined wealth of the bottom ninety-five percent. A snapshot look at 1998 shows that the top-earning one percent had as much income as the one hundred million Americans with the lowest earnings; and while corporate executives' pay in 1980 was a "mere" forty-two times that of the average production worker, by 1998 the figure grew to 419 times!

***

THERE IS CURRENTLY no shortage of criticism of this absolutely catastrophic situation. A threat to creature comforts and useless luxuries, though born essentially of "credit" that has no real existence, will make even the most uninterested howl with rage. What is absent, however, and what Belloc herein offers, is a solution.

That no solution will be forthcoming from anywhere else is obvious from the alternatives with which we are even now presented by those proposing to remedy the situation. Some suggest "restoring the New Deal," a socialist scheme attractive to some because of the evils that the "free market" itself had produced, but, more accurately, an opportunity for others to accomplish in one stroke an unprecedented expansion of government power and centralization, the final steps of which would no doubt be played out in any "New Deal II." Still others propose more of what lies essentially at the root of the economic disorder: "greater freedom and limited government in the spirit of Smith and Jefferson," as Milton Friedman suggests in his 1990 book, *Free to Choose*.

No, it is only the true Catholic, the heir of both true philosophy and sound economic practice, who offers not merely *a* third way, but *the* only way; a solution to the crisis which stems ultimately from what Devas, in his *Political Economy*, calls "the disastrous separation of economics from ethics, [which] was to be expected with the decay of philosophy, the loss of the sense of the unity of science, and the corresponding separation of political science from ethics."

Belloc, however, sees that unity of philosophy and the sciences; and for him it is a unity that is also historical. Belloc is still very much the historian, even in the present *Essay*. He knows that it is the moderns who reject the wisdom of history in continuing to defend the "unlimited freedom of struggle among competitors" which Pius XI correctly condemned as leading to the "concentration of power and might, the characteristic mark, as it were, of contemporary economic life" (*QA*, §107). It is rather the Distributists who articulate the programs which are compatible with human nature, and correspond to the common practice of mankind: a practice of the defense of the small property owner from economic extinction, "by the setting up of institutions for the protection of small property...institutions [that] have never broken down of themselves, but always and only under the conscious action of a deliberately hostile attack."

That attack began, as Belloc says, with "the destruction of the Guilds, coupled with the seizure of collegiate property in all countries transformed by the Reformation." It is an attack that continues to our day, intentionally on the part of a few, but mostly by force of habit on the part of those born into a system in which "completely free rein [is] given to human passions" (*QA*, §133).

It was to remedy this state of things that Belloc and his colleagues enunciated and defended the Distributist Vision, and for which aim we are now pleased to present Belloc's masterful *Essay*. We may be permitted to hope that its re-issue will contribute in some small way to a *Restoration* of not only property, but also of that conception of economic life which subordinates money and wealth to both the true needs of man and to the true Order which is Divine.

The Directors, IHS Press
August 15, 2002
Feast of the Assumption of
the Blessed Virgin Mary

"There is a third form of society, and it is the only one in which sufficiency and security can be combined with freedom, and that form is a society in which property is well distributed and so large a proportion of the families in the State severally OWN and therefore control the means of production as to determine the general tone of society; making it neither Capitalist nor Communist, but Proprietary."

Preface

HE "Essay on the Restoration of Property" which is here put before the reader, requires a word or two by way of preliminary, lest it should be misunderstood.

It will be noticed in the first place, that I have not dealt with the matter as a general, but as a particular, problem. I have discussed only opportunities for restoring property in modern England. I have given my reasons for so restricting the field. With English society affording today an extreme example of the destruction of property as an institution, to show the possibility of its restoration here is to show the possibility of its restoration anywhere.

Another and more practical reason is that in writing of England the writer has a concrete subject with which he is better acquainted than he is with the conditions of other countries.

It is therefore not a waste of effort or a provincial anomaly to consider the case of England by itself; for what is true of England in the matter is applicable to any less capitalistic society. My arguments apply, for instance, to Belgium, on its industrialized side, although in Belgium there is a large body of popular ownership remaining, and a strong peasantry which needs no revival.

Some may criticize me for not discussing the social and political arguments against small ownership. Its dangers and drawbacks are considerable and certainly deserve weighing against its advantages. Property, or management, concentrated in few hands, is used with greater knowledge and under better opportunities for large developments. A society of small owners may be over conservative and timid, probably more ignorant, than an economic oligarchy controlling its mass of wage slaves. In Foreign Affairs it is less likely to judge wisely and act rapidly. It may well be suspicious of new inventions and clumsy and recalcitrant at adapting itself to the use of new instruments. The reason I have not dealt with these aspects of the proprietary state, where a determining number of families are economically free, nor with the corresponding moral advantages of freedom and its frequent practical advantages, is that in so small a compass I desired to confine myself to the one issue of how such a freedom can be recovered. That simple issue would be confused if other considerations were intruded. It is as though one were discussing how life may be restored by artificial breathing, though well knowing that life may be a grievous burden.

Another point in which the reader may think me guilty of omission is the absence of any full discussion upon the new schemes of Social Credit. I have just touched on them in the last section of the essay, but only very briefly. My reason is this: that such schemes (notably the chief one, the Douglas Scheme[1]) do not directly advance, nor are directly connected with the idea of *property*. They are only connected with the idea of *income*. They propose, especially the Douglas Scheme of credit, to restore purchasing power to the destitute masses of society ruined by industrial capitalism.

That is exactly what a good distribution of property would also do; but a credit scheme could, in theory at least, do the thing at once and universally, while the restoration of property is unlikely to be achieved, and must, however successful, be a long business, spread over at least a couple of generations. Further, no restoration of property could be universal, applying to the whole of society equally.

The object of those who think as I do in this matter is not to restore purchasing power but to restore economic freedom. It is true that there cannot be economic freedom without purchasing power and it is true that economic freedom varies in some degree directly with purchasing power; but it is not true that purchasing power is equivalent to economic freedom. A manager at £1,000 a year who may get the sack at the caprice of his master has plenty of purchasing power, but he has not economic freedom. I do not avoid discussion of the new credit schemes, either from ignorance of them or from underestimating their high importance, but only because they are not to my purpose. If you are trying to persuade people to live on land instead of on the water you need not add a chapter on the art of swimming.

Further, it will appear that I propose no general scheme for restoring freedom and property. This may, indeed, be called a capital defect. All Reform depends upon some clear doctrine postulated and developed. No reform (it would seem) can hope to prosper which does not advance a programme covering all the field. I have not attempted to do so. For instance, though I have spoken much of distributing shares in corporate enterprise, I have spoken little of machinery whereby the holder of few shares could be given some real control over the policy which his company pursues.

Now my reason for such slight dealing with such a major problem is that I believe it, today, insoluble by general means. The evil has gone so far that, though the preaching of a new doctrine is invaluable, the creation of new and effective immediate machinery is impossible. The restoration of property must essentially be the product of a new mood, not of a new scheme. It must grow from seed planted in the breast. It is too late to reinfuse it by design, and our effort must everywhere be particular, local, and, in its origins at least, small.

Lastly, I must say a word here on something which appears more than once in the course of this essay, and that is my strong doubt upon the possibility of restoring property at all when it has once thoroughly disappeared.

It is customary in presenting any political thesis to include an element of hope. Professional politicians always make a point of prophesying success and even more respectable and sincere reformers love to exaggerate the chances of their ideal and even affirm its ultimate victory as certain. This has always seemed to me great folly. Wisdom consists in the appreciation of reality. If you approach a most difficult task under the illusion or the pretence that it is less difficult you may strengthen your supporters by the drug of illusion but you weaken them much more by persuading them to work in the void.

Respect for reality compels me to say that the Restoration of Property, when that institution has all but disappeared, is a task *almost* impossible of achievement. If it were *quite* impossible of achievement it would not be worthwhile wasting breath or ink upon. It is not *quite* impossible of achievement; at least, it is not quite impossible to start the beginnings of a change. But the odds against a reconstruction of economic freedom in a society which has long acquired the practice and habit of wage slavery is difficult beyond any other political task.

I do not know whether it be possible to start even the beginnings of a change. I doubt heavily that it is possible to plant successfully even the small seedlings of economic freedom in our society, here, in England, today.

What I certainly know is that failing such a change, our industrial society must necessarily end in the restoration of slavery. The choice lies between property on the one hand and slavery, public or private, on the other. There is no third issue.

HILAIRE BELLOC
King's Land,
February, 1936.

I

AN, TO LIVE, MUST TRANSFORM HIS ENVIROMENT from a state in which it is less to a state in which it is more useful to himself. This process is called "The Production of Wealth."

Moreover, if a man is to live conformably to his nature, there must be available for his consumption a certain amount of wealth, in a certain variety, for a certain unit of time. For instance, in our society, he must have so much bread, so much meat, so much of a number of different foods every day, so much beer or wine or spirits (or, if he be too weak to consume these) so much tea or coffee or what not; a sufficient amount of somewhat complicated clothing, all to last over such and such an amount of time; and a sufficiency of fuel, housing and all the rest of it, also to last a certain time.

Now this transformation of environment called "The Production of Wealth" is obviously only possible through the use of the instruments of production. A family can only live conformably to its human nature (that is, without undue suffering) in a given civilization on condition that it receive securely and constantly so much of this varied wealth for its consumption. But the wealth can only come into existence through the manipulating of natural forces by certain instruments; and there must also be an existing store of food and clothing and housing and the rest of it so that human beings may carry on during the process of production. These stores of wealth, these instruments and these natural forces are the *Means of Production*. It is obvious that whoever controls the means of production controls the supply of wealth. If, therefore, the means for the production of that wealth which a family needs are in the control of others than the family, the family will be dependent upon those others; it will not be economically free.

The family is ideally free when it fully controls all the means necessary for the production of such wealth as it should consume for normal living.

But such an ideal is inhuman and, therefore, not to be fixedly attained, because man is a social animal. It is not impossible of achievement for a short time, and has been briefly achieved whenever a lonely settler has fixed himself with his family and his stores in an isolated spot. But such complete economic freedom for each family cannot be permanent, because the family increases and divides into further numerous families, forming a larger community. Moreover, even were the isolated free family to endure, it would fall below the requirements of human nature, its isolation stunting and degrading it. For men cannot fulfill themselves save through a diversity of interests and ideas. Multiplicity is essential to life, and man to be truly human must be social.

Society being necessary to man, there arise in the economic field these two limitations to economic freedom:—

First, Difference of Occupation: Each in a society will concentrate upon what he has the best opportunity for producing and, by exchanging his surplus of it for that which another has the best opportunity of producing, will increase the wealth of all: or what comes to the same thing, lessen the burden of labour for all. Thus men live more happily in an agricultural village if there be a miller to grind the wheat instead of every family grinding it under their own roof, a cobbler to mend and make boots – and so on.

Second, A Principle of Unity: There must exist in some form the State. A sufficiently large unit for the development of the Arts and the better complexities of life must be organized. Its power must be appealed to for the satisfaction of justice, the prevention of internal disorder and for the arrangement of defence against external aggression. In general the State must exercise some restraint upon the ideal economic freedom of the family or freedom itself cannot be guaranteed.

But, while difference of occupation restricts the ideal independence of the family, it does not destroy freedom until one or another differentiated (and necessary) occupation can withhold its necessary function and thus impose its will. If the miller can refuse to supply flour to the rest, who have lost their instruments and aptitude for grinding wheat, he will be their master. So with the unifying authority of the State. If the State can cut off livelihood from the family, it is their master, and freedom has disappeared.

Therefore, there is a test of the limit after which such restriction of freedom is hostile to our aims and that test lies in the power of the family to re-act against that which limits its freedom. There must be a human relation between the family and those forces which, whether through the division of labour or the action of the State, restrict the family's liberty of choice in action. The family must have not only power to complain against arbitrary control external to it, but power to make its complaint effective.

It has been found in practice (that is, it is discoverable through history) that economic freedom thus somewhat limited satisfies the nature of man, and at the basis of it is the control of the means of production by the family unit. For though the family exchange its surplus, or even all its production, for the surplus of others, yet it retains its freedom, so long as the social structure, made up of families similarly free, exercises its effect through customs and laws consonant to its spirit: the Guild; a jealous watch against, and destruction of, monopoly; the safeguarding of inheritance, especially the inheritance of small patrimonies. The freehold miller, in such a society as was ours not so long ago, though he had no arable or pasture, was a free man. The yeoman, though he got his flour from the miller, was a free man.

The name for control of the Means of Production is "Property." When that control is exercised severally by individual units we call it "Private Property" to distinguish it from property vested in public bodies. When so great a number of families in the State possess Private Property in a sufficient amount as to give its colour to the whole, we speak of "widely distributed property."

It has been found in practice, and the truth is witnessed to by the instincts in all of us, that such widely distributed property as a condition of freedom is necessary to the normal satisfaction of human nature. In its absence general culture ultimately fails and so certainly does citizenship. The cells of the body politic are atrophied and the mass of men have not even, at last, an opinion of their own, but are moulded by the few who retain ownership of land and endowments and reserves. So property is essential to a full life, though it is debatable whether a full life is to be aimed at. There may be some who dislike freedom for themselves. There are certainly many who dislike it for others, but, at any rate, freedom involves property.

Today in England, and to a less degree in many other countries, widespread property has been lost. Ownership is not a general feature of society, determining its character. On the contrary, absence of ownership, dependence on a precarious wage at the will of others is the general feature of our society and determines its character.

The family does not possess that freedom which is necessary for its full moral health and that of the State of which it is the unit. Hence our society has fallen into the diseased condition known as "Industrial Capitalism." In this state the control of the Means of Production is vested in a comparatively small number; consequently economic freedom has ceased to be the note, giving its tone to society.

"Capitalism" does not mean a state of society in which capital has been accumulated, its accumulations protected, and itself put to use in producing wealth. Capital so accumulated, protected and used *must* exist in any human society whatsoever, including, of course, a Communist one. Nor does "Capitalism" mean a state of society in which capital is owned as private property by the citizens. On the contrary, such a society of free owners is the opposite of Capitalism as the word is here used. I use the term "Capitalism" here to mean a state of society in which a minority control the means of production, leaving the mass of the citizens dispossessed. Such a dispossessed body of citizens is called a "Proletariat."

Industrial Capitalism has in its present phase other grave evils attached to it besides the loss of freedom, for the twin evils of Insecurity and Insufficiency are attached to it. The main body of citizens, the Proletariat, are not sufficiently clothed, housed and fed, and even their insufficient supply is unstable. They live in a perpetual anxiety.

Now those two evils of insecurity and insufficiency might be eliminated and yet economic freedom be absent from the mass of society.

There are two ways in which they could be eliminated without the restoration of freedom:—

The first way is through that which I have called elsewhere "The Servile State." In this form of society the minority controlling the means of production supports all the vast majority of the dispossessed, even those whom it does not use in exploitation, and thus forms a stable society though one from which freedom is eliminated. That is the direction in which we are drifting today. The capitalists keep men alive by exploiting them at a wage, and when they cannot do this, still keep them alive in idleness by some small subsidy.

The second way is Communism – of its nature unstable but practicable at a heavy strain though, presumably, for only a comparatively short space of time. Under this second system the means of production are controlled by the officers of the

State, who are the masters of all the workers (slaves of the State), and the wealth produced is distributed, at the discretion of the State officials, among the families, or, if an attempt be made to abolish even the family, then among the individuals of the community.

There is a third form of society, and it is the only one in which sufficiency and security can be combined with freedom, and that form is *a society in which property is well distributed and so large a proportion of the families in the State severally* OWN *and therefore control the means of production as to determine the general tone of society;* making it neither Capitalist nor Communist, but Proprietary. If, then, we regard economic freedom as a good, our object must be thus to restore property. We must seek political and economic reforms which shall tend to distribute property more and more widely until the owners of sufficient Means of Production (land or capital or both) are numerous enough to determine the character of society.

But is economic freedom a good?

Unless we regard it as a good the search for methods by which property may be restored is futile or harmful. Indeed, as we shall see in a moment, unless a sufficient number of our fellow citizens feel with a sufficient degree of intensity that economic freedom is a good, economc freedom (that is, well-divided property) can never be restored.

So it behoves us at the outset to consider this question, whether or not economic freedom is a good.

Economic freedom can only be a good if it fulfills some need in our nature.

Now there is discoverable in man, Freewill. His actions are of moral value to him if they are undertaken upon his own initiative; not if they are undertaken under compulsion. Therefore the use of choice is necessary to human dignity. A man deprived of choice is by that the less a man, and this we all show through the repugnance excited in us by unauthorized restraint and subjection, through coercion rather than authority, to another's will. We cannot do good, or even evil, unless we do it freely; and if we admit the idea of good at all in human society, freedom must be its accompaniment.

Next, economic freedom is a good because man's actions are multiple, both his desires and his creative faculties; but it is only in the possession of economic freedom that this multiplicity can be effective. Deprived of economic freedom the units of society, the family and in some degree the individual, lack the power to express that diversity which is life. In the absence of economic freedom there must weigh upon any human society a dead and mechanical uniformity, increasingly leaden, and heavy and stifling, in proportion to the absence of freedom.

To all this two answers may be given by those who dread that restoration of property, or those who regard it as impossible.

First, it may be said that men do have economic freedom under State ownership. Secondly, it may be said that economic freedom, though a good, is of no moment in comparison with material satisfaction.

As to the first answer: It has been widely said in the recent past that economic freedom can exist without the institution of property, because, under a Communist system, men own though they own corporately: they can dispose of their own lives, though such disposition be indirect and through delegates. This false argument is born of the dying Parliamentary theory of politics; it proceeds from the false statement which deceived three generations of Europe, from the French Revolution to our own day, that corporate action may be identified with individual action. So men speak of their so-called "Representatives" as having been "chosen" by themselves. But in experienced reality there is no such thing as this imagined permanent corporate action through delegation. On some very simple and universal point, which all understand, in which all are interested and on which all feel strongly, the desire of the bulk of people may be expressed for a brief moment by delegation. Men voting under strong emotion on one single clear issue, may instruct others to carry out their wishes; but the innumerable acts of choice and expression which make up human life can never work through a system of delegation. Even in the comparatively simple field of mere political action, delegation destroys freedom. Parliaments have everywhere proved irreconcilable with democracy. They are not the people. They are oligarchies, and those oligarchies are corrupt because they pretend to a false character and to be, or to mirror, the nation. They are in reality, and can only be, cliques of professional politicians; unless, indeed, they are drawn from an aristocratic class which the community reveres. For class government, the product of the aristocratic spirit, is the condition of oligarchies working successfully and therefore of a reasonably efficient Parliament. Such an instrument is not to be found save in the hands of a governing class.

If this be true of mere politics it is obviously true of that millioned affair, our daily lives. Ownership by delegation is a contradiction in terms.

When men say, for instance (by a false metaphor), that each member of the public should feel himself an owner of public property – such as a Town Park – and should therefore respect it as his own, they are saying something which all our experience proves to be completely false. No man feels of public property that it is his own; no man will treat it with the care or the affection of a thing which is his own; still less can a man express himself through the use of a thing which is not his own, but shared in common with a mass of other men.

As to the second answer: It is said by many today that the satisfaction of man's immediate material necessities is on a different and infinitely more important plane than the satisfaction of his need for freedom. Economic freedom, if indeed it be a good at all, is (they say) a good of a much lesser sort, intangible, and something which men can well do without; therefore, since the enjoyment of it imperils the obtaining of material necessities, it must give way to that much greater good: a secure sufficiency of livelihood.

There is in this reply a measure of truth which gives it all its strength. It is half true; but the falsehood attached to the half truth vitiates the whole statement.

Where urgent material necessities are unsatisfied they must be satisfied first. Shipwrecked men on a raft at sea must live, exceptionally, under Communism. The dispossessed in a capitalist society must at least be kept alive. But it is not true that, such exceptional remedies for an unnatural evil having been used, we must go on to destroy the good of economic freedom for the advantage of enjoying greater material wealth.

This last argument is one of the many which we find in common to those who defend the Capitalist system and those who defend the Communist system: for Socialism and Capitalism are twin successive products of the same false philosophy.

The defenders of Capitalism tell us that it may have destroyed men's economic freedom; under Capitalism a man can less and less choose what he wants nor express his personality and character in the arts; but at least Capitalism has given him in far greater numbers a far greater mass of material goods than he had before it arose. The Communist goes one better. He says, "Yes: and under *my* system, by suppressing economic freedom altogether we shall give him yet more material goods, and we shall see that everybody gets them in almost unlimited amount."

If it were indeed true that economic freedom could not co-exist with a great deal of production, and still less with a sufficient distribution, it would still be worthwhile for those of our temper to sacrifice some portion of the material good, and even more worthwhile to permit inequality in distribution, for the sake of the economic freedom. But the truth is, as we shall see later on, that the supposed conflict between freedom and abundance, between freedom and a general enjoyment of that abundance, is an illusion born of Capitalism. It is an illusion which arises from the fact that the men who cherish it have so lived under a capitalist system all their lives that they can conceive of no alternative save a further development of it into Communism.

There remains indeed one answerable reply of objection. It is that of the man who says, "This or that, which economic freedom endangers, is a greater good in my eyes than is such freedom." For instance, he may think the military glory of the State a greater good, or magnificence on the part of the few a greater good. To such an objection we can only reply that our tastes differ and that we prefer freedom.

Economic freedom is in our eyes a good. It is among the highest of temporal goods because it is necessary to the highest life of society through the dignity of man and through the multiplicity of his action, in which multiplicity is life. Through well-divided property alone can the units of society react upon the State. Through it alone can a public opinion flourish. Only where the bulk of the cells are healthy can the whole organism thrive. It is therefore our business to restore economic freedom through the restoration of the only institution under which it flourishes, which institution is Property. The problem before us is, how to restore Property so that it shall be, as it was not so long ago, a general institution.

Three provisos must be kept clearly in mind before we approach the problem and attempt its practical solution.

The first proviso is that in the restoration of property we are not attempting, and could never reach, a mechanical perfection. We are only attempting to change the general tone of society and restore property as a commonly present, not a universal, institution.

The second proviso is that we cannot even begin such a reform unless there is a favourable state of mind present in society, a desire to own property, sufficient to support and maintain the movement and to nourish institutions which will make it permanent.

The third proviso is that in this attempt to restore Economic Freedom, the powers of the State must be invoked.

The first proviso is, I say, that, unlike the Servile State and unlike the Communist State, the Proprietary State does not present an ideal solution. There can be no perfection about it;

it must remain incomplete: nor could there be a better proof that the attempt is a human one, consonant to human nature.

To establish the Servile State one has but to follow certain lines which lead rapidly to an ideal conclusion, a society where *all* men, the few Capitalists and the mass of proletariat are *all* securely nourished – the latter on a wage, or, lacking this, a subsidy in idleness. The same is true with regard to the Communist State: a society where *all* men are securely nourished as slaves of the government. A simple formula and its exact application will, in each case, produce the ideal society envisaged.

In the first case all that is needed to produce the complete Servile State is a series of laws whereby every family – or every individual, if the family be eliminated – shall receive at least so much wealth as will maintain a certain standard of comfort and leisure; this minimum being provided for the dispossessed out of the stores controlled by the possessors. It will be distributed either in the form of wages, that is, the granting to the dispossessed by the possessors of some portion of the wealth which the dispossessed are producing by leave of the possessors; *or*, in the case of those who cannot be so employed, of relief during their enforced idleness.

This is the simple ideal of society to which we, in modern England, are advancing with great rapidity; indeed we have almost reached it.

The Possessors alone remain to enjoy economic freedom, the dispossessed – the very great majority – are deprived of it; but there is already at least security of *some* revenue for nearly all, and there can, with proper organization, be sufficiency for all as well. The only good lost to the masses, if it be a good, is freedom. For in such a state of society (the Servile State) the determining note is lack of freedom: the determining mass of society have no experience of economic liberty. The master class directs and is free: but society thinks and acts in terms of wage earners. The masses are kept alive, they are taught by a subsidy in childhood, treated by a subsidy in illness, and maintained by a subsidy in old age, widowhood and incapacity from accident. Soon no one of them may be suffering either hunger or cold or lack of any plain material necessity consonant to the type of civilization in which they live. But their activities are at the mercy of their masters.

Under the Communist scheme the matter is simpler still. It being made an offence for any man to own, all right to the use of accumulation by a family or an individual being destroyed, and all right of inheritance being also destroyed, the whole produce of the community is available for distribution to all. And Economic Freedom has disappeared for all through the action of a very few and simple but absolute coercive laws.

The formulae of the two schemes have been put in the past very well by the late Mr. Orage,[2] in words which appeared some 20 or 30 years ago in *The New Age*. I have not the exact phrases by me, but their sense is as follows:—

"Imagine a condition of affairs in which one machine is capable of producing all that society requires. Let that machine (and the natural forces) be under the control of one man. He is then the Capitalist of an ideally perfect Industrial Capitalist System. He will employ directly in industry as many men as may be required to work the machine. They will receive sustenance in the form of wages. He will also employ sundry other men, not directly in producing wealth with the machine, but ministering to his enjoyment; they may paint for him, print books for him, act plays for him, supply his domestic wants, and so forth. The rest will be unemployed. But as society would never be stable if the rest were to be condemned to death by starvation, laws will appear which demand by taxation, or customs will appear which demand by voluntary organization, so much of the produce of the machine as is necessary to support the unemployed. But these will not have the determining of what they are to receive, for they are not possessors. Their subsistence is doled out to them without their having discretion in the matter. And that is the Servile State. Or imagine the machine, and the material forces to which it is to be applied, controlled, not by one possessor, the Capitalist, but by the officers of the community, who shall at their discretion employ or dole out to each from the production of the machine; *then* you have the Communist State."

But the Proprietary State, the state of society such as our ancestors enjoyed, in which property is well distributed, does not admit of this simplicity, nor, being human, of this mechanical perfection. Property being a personal and human institution, normal to man, will always be, and must be, diversified. There is no advantage moral or social in land and capital being exactly distributed and there is no possibility of their being universally distributed. It would suffice for the health of the State by the Restoration of Property if, at the end of the reforming process, so many families were found possessed of property (in a sufficient amount) to give their tone to the State; just as today the wage earner and salary earner, the proletarians of every grade, give *their* proletarian tone to the State. The proletarians today vary in the degree of their dispossession, some have only the clothes they stand in, others a little furniture as well, others some further small insufficient accumulation – a few shares, or a mortgaged house or what not – but the note which they strike, the character which they impress upon society, is that of a wage-earning State rapidly turning into a Servile State.

But whereas the Servile State to which we are now tending can be complete, the Proprietary (or Distributist) State neither can, nor should be, complete; for it cannot of its nature be mechanical. There will be many comparatively poor, and some comparatively rich. There will presumably be some proportion of dispossessed. But Property, and its accompaniment, Economic Freedom, will be the mark of society as a whole.

The second proviso, that we can do nothing unless there is a state of mind favourable to us, may seem to make the whole effort futile. The state of society in which we are now living in England has largely forgotten what property is. Men talk in terms of employment and wages. When they talk of ownership the word calls up in their minds the ownership of large property by a few. Whether there remains today in England a desire for economic freedom (that is, for property) sufficient to nourish the beginnings of a change, nothing but experiment can decide. Increase of revenue, not ownership, is the object of most men. Ownership is certainly not the object of *most* men; if it were, there would have been successful protest long ago against the wage-earning system.

As we all know, there was some confused protest at the beginning of the Industrial Revolution and throughout its earlier stages; there was violence used to try and prevent the enclosure of the commons and there were riots against the new machines. But that was a long time ago. Take the process as a whole, from the first step, the great confiscation of corporate property in the sixteenth century, through the Statute of Frauds in the seventeenth century, when a mass of small yeomen were dispossessed, follow it on to the mid-nineteenth century, and you do not find at any stage a clear determination to maintain well-divided property, nor even a widespread instinct in its favour. It was because such a spirit was lacking that Capitalism came upon us. In countries where that spirit was present, though Capitalism has also taken root there, it has never flourished in the same way, it has always been handicapped.

But though the appetite for private property has weakened, though it is not present as yet in the mass of the wage-earning population, its relics may *possibly* prove, if the first experiments can be undertaken, sufficiently alive to leaven the whole body of society gradually. It *may* be possible to "re-plant" property even in England, just as one can re-afforest poor ground by taking advantage of exceptional patches, establishing the new growth there, sheltering its beginnings, and leaving it to propagate itself when it shall have sufficient strength. Only, what we must not trust to is the mere machinery of reform. Of its nature property is the product of human desire; we can help on that desire to achieve its fulfilment, but we cannot create it. We cannot make owners by merely giving men something to own. And, I repeat, whether there be sufficient desire for property left upon which we can work, only experience can decide.

The third proviso, that we must call in the State to help us, should present no difficulties save to minds misled by the false categories of the nineteenth century – by such terms as "Individualism," for instance, which never did or could correspond to reality.

The evil from which we are suffering today is not the evil of State interference but the evil of the loss of Freedom. State interference may have for its effect a loss of Freedom and certainly usually has for its object the loss of Freedom; but it always may be, and very often must be, invoked for the very purpose of restoring Freedom. There must be laws to protect property not only against direct rapine but against dissolution through the exaggeration of competition. There must be State sanction for the powers of the Guild, for the process of Inheritance, for the restriction of undue burdens. There must be some official machinery for fostering the propagation of small property just as there is official machinery today fostering the destruction of small, widespread property by large owners: and the effort at restoring property will certainly fail if it is hampered by a superstition against the use of force as the handmaid of Justice. All the powers of the State have been invoked by Capitalism to restore servile conditions; we shall not react against servile conditions unless we avail ourselves of the same methods.

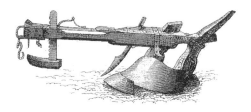

II

S WE APPROACH THE PROBLEM OF THE RESTORA-
tion of property there are two main principles to
be kept in mind:—

(i) The first is that *any effort to restore the institution
of property* (that is, re-establish a good distribution of property
in a proletarian society such as ours has become) *can only be successful through a deliberate reversal of natural economic tendencies.*

(ii) The second is that *our effort will fail unless it be accompa-
nied by regulations making for the preservation of private property,
so much of it as shall have been restored.*

Both of these principles are essential to success. As I have
said, without a sufficient desire for property present in a sufficient number of people, the attempt cannot succeed anyhow.
But however strong that desire, and however widespread, the
effort will also fail if these two principles are not concurrently
observed.

I have compared the restoration of property in a society
such as ours, where it has been ruined, to the re-afforestation
of land.

Another parallel is the reclamation of swamp. Natural
tendencies have made a piece of land marshy. It lies low, the
rainfall is heavy, the soil impervious and sticky. To reclaim
it you must act *against* natural tendency. You must drain, cut
channels, embank; and having done so, you must see to it that
the banks, drains and channels shall be maintained against the
constant effort of nature to drag the land back to swamp again.

So it is with property. Property, as a general social institution, well-divided property, having disappeared and Capitalism having taken its place, you cannot reverse the process without acting *against* natural economic tendencies. Well-divided property will not spring up of itself in Capitalist society. It must be artificially fostered. Communism will spring up of itself and flourish in Capitalist society, for it is a product of Capitalist thought and moves along the same lines as Capitalism. But well-divided property will not so arise.

Moreover, once restored, Property must be constantly sustained or it will lapse again into Capitalism.

Private property acting unchecked, that is, in the absence of all safeguards for the preservation of the small man's independence, tends inevitably to an ultimate control of the means of production by a few; that is, in economics, to Capitalism and therefore, in politics, to Plutocracy.

At this point I must introduce a digression to meet two objections which will be made by any socialist reader upon his hearing this admission (as he would call it) on my part. For whether a man be a socialist enthusiastically (because he believes communal property to be the most just economic arrangement) or whether he is a socialist reluctantly (because he believes that communal control, though odious, is the lesser of two evils and the only alternative to control by a few rich men), takes it for granted that industrial capitalism was ultimately *inevitable* wherever private property was a social institution.

On reading, I say, this which he would call an "admission" on our side, that private property unchecked by special preservative conditions lapses into Capitalism and all its evils, he may consider that since the defenders of property are agreed it must be so, further discussion is a waste of time. Or he may be one of those who say, "perhaps private property could have been restored under simpler conditions, but in modern society, with its use of machinery and its rapidity of communication, it is too late to make the attempt."

Both these positions are erroneous.

The first, which is the commonest and which we hear on every side, all around us, is based upon the two main characteristics of modern political thought, false history and a false philosophy. The idea that Capitalism arose of itself, and necessarily, from the mere institution of private property, is the fruit of bad history pressed into the service of bad philosophy.

It is not true that Capitalism arose inevitably from the necessary development of economic institutions under the doctrine of private property. Capitalism only arose *after* the safeguards guaranteeing well-distributed property, private property, had been deliberately broken down by an evil will insufficiently resisted. It was not Capitalism that came first and gradually dissolved the institution of well-divided property; it was the conditions under which alone well-divided property could survive, and had survived for centuries, which were first destroyed. Only then, after their destruction, was the field free for the growth of plutocracy in politics and Capitalism in the economic structure of the State. There was something of a proletariat before this great revolution took place. There were landless men, many of them, by the end of the Middle Ages, and there were already many men working at transport and exchange, and in the Crafts, who had not enough property to count. But the point is that they did not give their tone to the State. They were not so numerous as to mark the character of society until the religious revolution of the sixteenth century had destroyed the ancient walls which had protected the freedom of the human city.

The first great blow was the destruction of the Guilds, coupled with the seizure of collegiate property in all countries transformed by the Reformation, but most thoroughly and universally in England. This was followed up in England by a series of positive enactments of which that one called the Statute of Frauds was perhaps the chief instrument in destroying the English land-owning peasantry.* The great efflorescence

---

* The Statute of Frauds, made law by the Big Landlords and the Lawyers' Guild under Charles II, after the breakdown of English Monarchy and the

of Capitalism came *after* all that bad work had been done, and was only made possible by that bad work.

Nor is it true that machinery in its various forms, including the modern conquest of space (rapidity of transport in material things and ideas) lies at the root of this modern evil. The machine does not control the mind of man, though it affects the mind of man; it is the mind of man that can and should control the machine.

Moreover, it is not true that the machine is necessarily a centralizer of effort; in some cases it is, in others it is not. The railway worked in favour of those who desired to centralize effort for their own advantage; it added a new support for an already founded capitalist system. But the internal combustion engine works the other way. It transports men and things in decentralized fashion, and it is at the command of the small man. The motor bus in the country was decentralizing the control of passenger traffic, and the lorry that of small goods traffic, when capitalist monopoly got to work and began to eat up the lesser units which were further persecuted by restrictive laws. Had a cumulative tax been clapped on to the ownership of more than a few vehicles licensed for country transport, a tax becoming high at half a dozen vehicles and prohibitive at a dozen, we should have continued the small property in transport that was growing up. Similarly steam factory machinery in the mid-nineteenth century and earlier could be used in favour of already established Capitalism and in a fashion hos-

---

beginning of aristocratic government in its place, provided, among other things, that no title to land should be valid unless there were written proof of the same. Now the mass of small English yeomen had no such documents to show. They held their land from father to son under the village landlord in fee-farm tenure, paying only small quit rents. They were thus owners and hereditary owners of their tenures by traditional and immemorial custom and hereditary free-holders. But, after the Statute of Frauds, the local village landlord could, and gradually did, claim ownership of the land and reduce this class of peasant to a tenant on a competitive rent, and a lease of only such length as the landlord chose to grant. He gradually sank to become a proletarian labourer.

tile to small property. But electrical power works just the other way. Its origin is more efficient if centralized, though there is no compulsion to centralize it; but its distribution may be infinitely varied and split up into the smallest units. Moreover, even where the modern instrument is expensive and therefore makes for centralization, it could be owned and worked as Guild property, or in distributed shares, well safeguarded.

The whole attitude of the old-fashioned socialist, or, as he has now logically become, the Communist, with his well-worn argument of inevitability, is rooted in a wrong conception of what men are − that is, a false philosophy − supported by a wrong conception of the historical process reached by the putting of events in the wrong historical order. And though it is true that unchecked competition must ultimately produce the rule of ownership by a few, yet it is also true that mankind has always felt this to be the danger, has instinctively safeguarded itself against that danger by the setting up of institutions for the protection of small property, and that these institutions have never broken down of themselves, but always and only under the conscious action of a deliberately hostile attack. So the carefully planned irrigation of the Tigris and Euphrates[3] combatted with success the natural tendency of the swamp and the desert till the Mongol deliberately destroyed such safeguards of civilization.

* * * *

THERE ARE SEVEN main avenues whereby unchecked competition tends to put a few into the control of the means of production, transport and exchange, and therefore of society as a whole. There are seven main ways whereby healthy normal human society with a mass of well-distributed ownership can degenerate into a Capitalist society, the mark of which is the exploitation of the many by the wealthy few, and the power of plutocracy over all.

These seven avenues may be tabulated as follows:—

1. The larger unit is in proportion less expensive than the smaller in management, rent, upkeep and all things that are called in commercial jargon "overhead charges." The only limit to this tendency is the difficulty of organizing and conducting units beyond a certain size; and that difficulty is more and more easily overcome by practice and the development of perfected organization.

2. The larger economic unit is better able to purchase all the more expensive instruments for production, distribution and exchange, whether in the form of machinery, advertizing or information – through which last, other things being equal, the richer man is possessed of a better basis for judgement than the poorer man.

3. The larger unit can borrow more easily *in proportion* than the smaller. It can especially tap bank credit more easily and bank credit is, today, the chief factor in economic activity of all kinds.

4. The larger institution can undersell the smaller one at a loss, until the smaller one is imperilled or killed. The richer man, or combination, can thus "rope in" the smaller man, or "freeze him out"; that is, compel him to alliance on onerous terms or actually destroy him.

5. The larger unit will accumulate capital under easier conditions than the smaller. The rich man feels less the privation of saving and can take as sufficient enticement a smaller profit or a lower interest on money than could compensate the poorer man for his sacrifice.

6. Plutocracy once established will corrupt the legislature so that laws will be made in its favour, increasingly handicapping the small man and advantaging the larger.

7. Plutocracy once established will equally corrupt the administration of justice, weighing the scales in favour of the rich man against the poor man.

Let us consider these seven dangers more particularly.

1. *The overhead charges.* This is one of the stock arguments of Communism, and a good one so far as it goes. The old

typical illustration used to be, in this country, the retail urban milk trade. Your Fabian[4] bewailed the state of affairs in which two small men, each with the goodwill of a milk walk, over-lapped. He pointed out that the expenses of distribution would be vastly reduced by one system controlling the whole mass of small milk walks as they existed not so long ago. He has lived to see the thing come about, in this country at least; for the small man in the milk trade has almost disappeared. But the mass of small free dealers in milk have not been merged in the Socialist State. They have become wage slaves. A huge monopoly has swallowed them up.

And what is true of the milk trade is true of all the other examples of distribution and of most of the examples of production. Chain shops have destroyed the individual shop-keeper. Where there were, say, forty thousand independent grocers, there came to be forty thousand managers, the wage slaves of a combine, because the cost of administration is less, and this economic advantage handicaps the small man against the great. It has gone on all around us during the past generation at a pace which has increased, in England at least, out of all knowledge, until today on all sides we are gripped by monopoly. Those of my generation can remember a time when for a hundred necessities of daily life individual shops or craftsmen were present throughout London. Today they are fast disappearing; most of them have already gone.

2. *Information.* In purchasing information for a correct judgement, the larger group of capital has an obvious advantage over the smaller. It is apparent in every economic activity, and in one department of it, the ease of negotiations, is perhaps more striking than the rest. You can make a merger of a few great firms and with that merger create a monopoly in what they produce or distribute, where you could not make a merger of a number of small firms. With such power admitted freely, working without check, monopoly is the inevitable term to which the whole process of competition tends.

Again, the large unit in modern scientific production – e.g., electrical – has a mass of technical experts and a quasi monopoly of informed ability in execution. To such, even a national government must perforce turn when great works are undertaken. The power of the larger unit to purchase the more expensive material instrument which the smaller units cannot purchase (save in combination) is also obvious; but it is not always equally apparent, as it should be, that the larger unit can more easily command another immaterial instrument of the greatest force: publicity. We all know that advertizing has become one of the worst plagues of English modern life; what we must also keep constantly before our eyes is that the opportunity for this abuse increases *out of all proportion with the increase of the unit at work.* £100,000 spent on advertizing has not 100 times the effect of £1,000 – it has much more than 1,000 times the effect.

It has been discovered that with a dull urban population, all formed under a mechanical system of State education, a suggestion or command, however senseless and unreasoned, will be obeyed if it be sufficiently repeated. Now, in issuing such suggestions and commands the larger man has an overwhelming advantage over the smaller. He can, as it were, compel by suggestion. He can create by it a market for his wares which the small man could never command and out of which the small man will be driven.

We all must remark and deplore the undoubted truth that this particular form of plutocratic advantage (I quote it only as an example, but I do so because it is the most glaring and offensive example of all) tends not only to establish a few rich men or small groups of masters in distribution and production, but also to produce and to distribute the worst things. Everyone must have noticed how an article deteriorates after an "advertizing campaign" has been started in its favour.

It is true that this particular evil would in time correct itself as the general evil of Capitalism increased, for when all is monopoly, even advertizing will not be required. But as things stand today, this fungoid growth of advertizing has done evil beyond anything which our fathers could have imagined. Undoubtedly it is the strongest of the forces which have so degraded our Press. The Press cannot print, even where it should so desire (and being itself in the hands of monopolists it does not so desire to print) any truth which the great advertizers desire to have suppressed. And that is why our field of vision, even on the most urgent public affairs, grows narrower and narrower.

3. What the power to obtain credit (especially, of course, bank credit) means today we shall discuss when we come to examine the part played by finance in industrial Capitalism; but we note here that the advantage enjoyed in this department by the larger unit is, again, as in the other instances given, out of proportion to the size of the units engaged. The small craftsman can hardly borrow at all – perhaps a few pounds privately at ruinous interest. The somewhat larger man can borrow more, in proportion, upon the security of his business, but he is not "interesting" to the banker. The owner – or controller – of a very large business can borrow on quite another scale. He does not command, say, ten times the credit of a rival with a tenth of his business; he commands twenty or thirty times the amount and on easier terms.

There are three main ways in which this advantage works:—

(a) The large unit can bargain for special rates of interest, lower than are granted to the smaller unit, because (1) the cost of "handling" the loan is proportionately less, (2) the transaction is unilateral in the case of the small man but mutual in the case of the large man. It does not matter much to the bank whether Jones the grocer is their client for £1,000, while it is life and death to Jones to get the money. He will pay, say, 8 or 10% in interest and "charges"; but even so it is hardly worth the bank's while to bleed him. But, it matters a great deal to the bank to have Sir Hannibal Smith for a client, with his loan of a million, bringing profit to the bank at the rate of £45,000 a year, or even only £40,000. And Sir Hannibal is fully aware of that fact.

(b) It may often "pay" the bank, in the case of the big man, to "throw good money after bad." It never pays the bank to do so in the case of the small man. *He* is sacrificed at once and his ample security is pouched by the Creditor. The bank is not unwilling to see him outed. He was becoming a nuisance. But with the Big Man it is otherwise. If the bankers sell the big man up, they lose a potential source of later income; so they try to "tide him over." We see the effects of this in mills which the banks supported through the Slump until they owed far more than they were worth; and of large commercial men whose private households are actually paid for week by week out of the banks resources, because the banks find, or think they find, it to their advantage to keep them afloat.

(c) A subtle point, but a very real one: the large client is in the same "atmosphere" as the bank. They are both "Big Business." The psychology of credit works here most powerfully in the very large man's favour, and the proof of this truth is seen in the numerous cases where, after a man in a large way has failed, bank credit has been discovered to have been put at his service upon his mere name or with quite insufficient security.

4. The large unit can undersell the smaller unit by fraud as well as by cheaper overhead charges. This is one of the oldest complaints against centralized capital and the worst of the big man's methods in his swallowing up the small man. It was one of the first evils of the growing capitalist system to be noted. It was already in full swing shortly after the middle of the nineteenth century. It is, of course, for all those who admit the doctrine of the Just Price, manifestly a form of theft.

It works thus:—The larger unit of capital can afford to lose on its wares for a longer time than the smaller unit. If both the larger and the smaller unit are producing a particular article at a pound, both in competition sell it at fifteen shillings, each will be losing five shillings on every sale. The process could not go on indefinitely, but the larger unit of capital can stand the loss longer than the smaller one. The small man will break, while the large man is still solvent. And this iniquitous method by which the large man destroys the small, is, in all its modifications and varied forms, not only one of the most obvious, but one of the most pernicious, activities of capitalism. It is also, as we shall see later, when we come to the question of restrictive prohibitions, one of the most difficult to deal with. For there are many conditions under which a man may honestly and in good faith sell at a loss, and to distinguish between these and the conditions under which he sells in order to ruin a competitor is difficult.

5. The larger unit of capital will automatically be accumulated for a lesser proportionate reward than the smaller one. *This is an exceedingly important point which the earlier critics of Capitalism overlooked. It is a major cause in the disastrous swelling of large accumulations and corresponding disappearance of small property and economic freedom.*

Capital accumulates for a certain reward. Capital is created by saving out of production for the purposes of future production, and it will not be so accumulated by anyone, the individual owner nor the Communist State, save for some standard of remuneration. A certain measure of this reward sufficient to provoke an accumulation of capital, produce what John Stuart Mill[5] called "the effective desire of accumulation," and we cannot do better than adopt this conventional term. Without "an effective desire of accumulation of Capital," either in the private citizen or in the direction of the Communist State, the stores of livelihood, the maintenance of instruments, and (of course) addition thereto will dwindle and fail, and wealth will decline. Men will not forego a present for a future good save on terms of increment. Whether as individuals, as families or as governments, men will not deprive themselves of the immediate enjoyment of a sum of wealth for the sake of a future sum of wealth, unless the second is larger than the first. A man certainly will not wittingly forego ten pounds worth of immediate enjoyment if he knows that at the end of the year he will have only the same ten pounds for his pains. He may not save that ten pounds if he knows that at the end of the year he will only have ten guineas. He will more probably do so if he sees eleven pounds at the end of the year. But at any rate he must have some increment as an incentive, and the amount of increment which will set him to work to save, the reward sufficient to make him forego immediate enjoyment, is the measure of his "effective desire of accumulation."

It is an error, as I have just said, to imagine that this factor is only present under Capitalism. It is necessarily present under Communism, or under well-divided property, and indeed in any economic system whatsover. Under Communism, for instance, the Government officials will not risk an added strain of want among their slaves unless there is prospect of later advantage. With well-divided property the point is obvious.

In general, then, Capital is accumulated with the purpose of future production in excess of its present amount, and if such addition were not expected, Capital would not be accumulated at all.*

Now, this being so, we note at once that the wealthy man (or controller of the larger unit) will feel an effective desire for accumulation for a smaller proportionate increment than will the poorer man. We put it conversationally when we say that it is worth a man's while to get £2,500 a year on £50,000 capital, but hardly worth his while to forego £1's worth of enjoyment in January in order to get a benefit of an extra shilling at the end of the year. Another way of putting it is to repeat the obvious truth that the margin for saving in the case of poor men is narrow, while that of rich men is wide. It is easier to save £5,000 a year out of £10,000 a year than to save £500 a year out of £1,000 a year. And out of £50 a year no man could save £25 (in England today) and keep alive. The poor man who saves "against a rainy day," who looks on his savings as a sum

---

* The replacement of Capital as it is consumed is not the same thing as accumulation. But it follows the same rules. A railway company repairs and restores its plant, not for extra profit, but to maintain the existing profit. So does the village carrier. But even maintenance involves foregoing immediate use, and such sacrifice is easier for the company than for the carrier.

to be called upon later for his maintenance, will often take very low interest rather than none. Often he will seek for none and merely leave his money on current account, if he has a bank, or to take the interest which a Capitalist government keeps ridiculously low in savings banks and certificates (in order not to compete with its wealthy supporters) or to keep it in a box. But when it comes to serious amounts sufficient to start a man independently, it is another matter. He will not make a venture at a livelihood as farmer or shopkeeper for an insignificant percentage of his savings.

In other words, you cannot tempt small capital to make the beginnings of serious accumulation at the rates which are sufficient for large capital. In order to get the small man to accumulate – in order, that is, to create well-distributed small capital through the serious accumulation of little savings – you must early begin to offer a proportionately higher reward than you do for large savings.

Unrestricted economic tendency works therefore to the advantage of large units in this case again. The cost of managing a quantity of little savings bank accounts, for instance, is out of all proportion greater than the cost of handling large balances and in point of fact we always find, in the modern capitalistic system, that the first small beginnings of savings are offered lower rewards than the larger ones. The Post Office gave no more than half the rate of the State after the war, and the Savings Certificates were calculated at a rate lower than that of the main national loans.

6. The effect of plutocracy in corrupting the legislative machine needs in theory no demonstration, for we all know nowadays that such corruption is ubiquitous, and nowhere does it work with greater force than under a parliamentary system. To have effect there is no necessity for actually handing over shares or money to the politicians (though a great deal of that simple form of corruption does take place) for even when such direct action of plutocracy upon the legislative machine is not exercised, there is indirect "pressure" of all

kinds. The evil is less formidable under active monarchy than under any other form of government, for the whole point of absolute monarchy is that the monarch is too wealthy to be bullied. But in all other forms of government the pressure of the whole wealthy class upon the legislative machine is felt, and when that wealthy class is supreme and has complete economic power over the mass of the citizens, laws will inevitably be made favouring the continuance of the system and handicapping the better distribution of property. Not only statutes, but all kinds of regulations and customs will conform to this rule.

There has also lately arisen a new form of "pressure." A large unit of production – say, electrical – pushes through Parliament some great public scheme, often to the material benefit of the nation, *but* so that the wealthy men who control the unit shall necessarily receive the profits on the large sums of public money expended, or, what comes to the same thing, enormous salaries paid out of the taxes.

7. The last noticeable effect of plutocratic pressure is that exercised upon the administration of justice. This again, in its cruder and simpler form is less dangerous than in its indirect form. Where the direct bribing of lawyers is eliminated there remain two powerful examples of plutocratic effects upon them. The first is the cost of obtaining justice; the second, the legislative effect of judicial decisions.

As to the first of these, we are today surrounded by it on every side. The cost of recovering the smallest debts is out of all proportion to the cost of recovering a large one. The scale of payments which have to be met before a citizen is enabled to have justice at all is higher in a plutocracy, such as ours, than under any other form of government. Justice in the matter of small sums is sold by the lawyers at a preposterous cost, and on larger sums is still very high through the cost of appeals. It is a mere commonplace that the wealthier unit can take a thing in this country to the ultimate Court of Appeal, the House of Lords, where the poorer rival cannot.

The effect of the same spirit upon judicial decisions has been evident through history during the last 350 years, and was particularly strong during the great confiscations of land. It was largely by judicial decisions, rather than by direct legislation, that the waste lands, the minerals, forests, commons and the rest, were stolen from the monarchy in the past, and handed over to its wealthier subjects. The thing began with the active decay of royal power under Elizabeth,[6] and continued through the seventeenth century.

Our first approach, then, to the problem must be the consideration of what remedies are available by way of check, modification or prohibition, for meeting these seven lines of attack along which large property advances in its ceaseless campaign for absorbing or attempting to absorb small property and to turn the small owner into a proletarian. To the consideration of those remedies I will now turn.

III

HE PRACTICAL PROBLEM BEFORE US IS HOW TO effect the beginnings, at least, of a restoration of property in this society of ours wherein property has been almost destroyed, its principles forgotten, and acquaintance with it lost in the determining majority of our fellow citizens.

The problem is one applying to this particular country – England – at this particular moment. We have to deal with it in a very different way from what we might adopt in a country where property was still for most men a desire, and for a further sufficient number of men a known experience.

We can only try to restore it as an experiment: only attempt to establish it in some measure. We can only sow the seeds of such a restoration in a country which has fallen prey to industrialized capitalism with a determining number of its citizens proletarian – that is, wage slaves.

Now, the obvious intellectual answer to the main question: "How shall we proceed?" is to discover the root of the evil and attack the root.

On the surface the cause of the evil would appear to be unchecked competition, with its destruction of all those safeguards whereby property maintained itself for centuries before the breakdown which began with the Reformation. But we can go deeper than that. The profound, ultimate root of the whole affair is a certain mood – an attitude of mind. Where you have a public opinion supporting well-divided property, a state of society which takes well-divided property for granted and therefore a philosophy consonant with well-divided property, institutions or customs conservative of property will arise of their own accord. Conversely, attacks upon the small owner, his attempted destruction by the great man, will be defeated.

"Therefore" (says the intellectual observer of the problem), "we can only effect even the beginnings of the mighty change we have in view by going to the very ultimate causes to apply our remedy there. We must change the philosophy, that is, the religion of the society in which we live. A false and poisonous philosophy having produced industrial capitalism with its herd of wage slaves, and having destroyed normal human economic freedom, we must re-establish a sane philosophy – or rather religion – whence right institutions would necessarily proceed. We must convert England to a right religion before we can make Englishmen free."

Well, this obvious and radical attitude, at the risk of paradox, I beg leave to challenge.

I do not think that in England as now constituted there is a chance of changing the minds of men from that philosophy whence all these evils have proceeded. Nor do I think that the enormous structure of industrial capitalism, with its establishment, as a dominating social feature, of a millioned proletariat in the place of free citizens, can be quickly overset by the propagation of ideals. This attempt at general conversion must go on all the time, side by side with the practical tackling of the problem, and such effort at conversion is itself practical; but at the moment we cannot expect from it effects on a scale worth noticing, and meanwhile society runs down steeply into the Servile State.

It is the conviction that a change of philosophy is not possible *in time to be of service*, which has decided most of those who have enough historical knowledge and enough moral sense to hate capitalism, and at the same time enough intelligence to despise Socialism, to stand aside or (or what comes to the same thing as standing aside) to discuss the abstract doctrine of economic freedom without attempting to issue a concrete programme for its re-creation. All around us everything works for the destruction of such small proportion of well-divided property as remains. Every unit in our social machinery, every habit of our thought takes the present perversion of civilization for granted. It takes it for granted that the only solution of our evils is a solution of the same nature as those evils, to wit, the Socialist solution. "We have lost," they say, "our economic freedom, and it is impossible to recover it." Or again, "since there must be monopoly and since the mass of men must be slaves of monopoly, let us at least put monopoly into the hands of the State and not leave it to a few millionaires."

To this objection I answer that, though certainly it is impossible to change a false philosophy in time to save the situation, yet there *may* be enough normal love of freedom remaining, however feeble, to be used as a starting point. There *may* be embers aglow here and there, sufficient to start the small beginnings of a flame.

It is, indeed, true that the position to be attacked is formidable. It is so formidable that anyone may be forgiven for regarding it as not only impregnable, but invulnerable. English industrial Capitalism with its clique of masters and its myriad of dependents, is a fortress against which any efforts we may make through attempted reforms of laws here and there, through attempted founding of new institutions here and there, might be compared to the attacking of one of the old-fashioned stone fortresses by unarmed men. They could hardly loosen a stone. They are surely impotent to effect any breach, however slight, in the invincible defence.

But when you are considering how a fortress may be attacked with the means at your disposal, it is your first business to ask yourself where its weak points are to be found. The weakness may seem slight, the opportunity of action against such great and highly organized strength may seem negligible, but the very first business is to find out, at least, *where* there is an opportunity, even on a small scale, for beginning. In other words, the practical thing is not to attempt to undermine industrial capitalism at once and as a whole – that can only be done by a change in the religion or philosophy of the citizens; nor even to attempt to make suddenly a great breach in the defence (for that could only be done with weapons we do not possess) but to seek out those points, however apparently insignificant, in which the reversal of the great process can be sporadically begun.

I would, therefore, in the consideration of a practical programme, set out the various points of that programme in an order almost exactly the opposite of the intellectual order, and would begin with the things that can be done even now, at once, with some chance of partial and limited success. The process may be compared to the killing of a tree by one who must attack with some instrument – say, shears – too feeble for cutting the tree down, let alone uprooting it; too feeble even for inflicting a serious wound upon its trunk; too feeble for cutting off main branches or perhaps secondary branches, *but not too feeble for clipping leaves.*

Now, if you cut enough leaves off a tree the tree dies; and a man not having an axe or a saw or a spade may yet with small shears and the slight aggressive power of his two hands begin to destroy one after the other the leaves. With this principle in mind, and for that purpose, I ask what concrete proposals are available for weakening Industrial Capitalism and its Socialist fruit. How can we, meanwhile, sow fresh seed, from whence the institution of property shall begin to re-arise?

There are three main departments in the problem: (a) the restoration of the small cultivator, distributor and craftsman, either as individual families or as employers in the human domestic word "employer" that is, dealing with but few and personally known subordinates; (b) the division of property in enterprises necessarily large, among many holders in sufficient amount; (c) the confirming of such wholesome division by institutions which shall maintain it and prevent a recurrent degradation of property into capitalism.

Before considering these three departments of our effort, a digression must be admitted upon the function of what is today called "The State"; what used to be called (in the days when men preferred reality) "The King."

We have already said that no such reformation as we are contemplating can be undertaken or continued without the use of State power. And to understand the necessity for this we must get rid of the false category whereby men think in terms of two contrasted methods which they call Socialism and Individualism.

These terms do not indicate a true contrast. There is no such thing as Individualism. An action by the State is one thing when it is used to free mankind and to give the citizens economic independence, and an exactly opposite thing when it is used to take that independence away. As men would have put it when property was, indeed, well-distributed and when it corresponded to a strong national monarchy, "the King is there to safeguard the freedom of the small man against the tyranny of the great." That is a King's main function, and there is nothing in common between the exercise of that function and the oriental idea of the King as universal owner with all men his slaves. On the contrary, the right conception of kingship as the moderator and preserver of freedom is the very contrary to, and destruction of, the wrong conception of kingship as a universal despotism. We shall find as we proceed in our search for Economic Freedom, that we cannot follow it for any distance without calling in the powers of the State, to contrast with, and as far as possible to destroy, the usurped powers of Big Business.

To return, then, to the concrete proposals for a remedy. We propose to re-establish the peasant, the craftsman and the small (and secure) retail tradesman.

The Peasant, as being by far the most important of all these and the foundation of all, I reserve to a separate chapter.

If we look at our present industrialized society we perceive, of the two other opportunities for particular action, the opportunity for restoring the small distributor (that is, the small shopkeeper) and the opportunity for restoring the small workshop (that is, the craftsman). The first is, under present English conditions, a much more promising opportunity than the second.

As to the restoration of the small distributor (or perhaps we may call it "the saving of him," for he still survives as a type with very numerous examples), there would seem to be two converse economic policies available together. The first is the handicapping of the large distributor, by differential taxation; the second is using such a system for the artificial economic protection of the small distributor – in both of which policies, of course, one must go directly contrary to the accepted doctrines of the past, which have led us into the mess where we are now floundering.

There are three forms of differential taxation on large distributors (I mean, of course, large retail distribution as it exists today in England), all three of which must be applied simultaneously. These three are Differential Taxation (1) against chain stores; (2) against multiple shops; (3) against large retail turnover.

(1) There must be a differential tax on chain shops, that is, on the system whereby one man or corporation controls a great number of different shops of the same kind. To control two such may involve but a small tax, to control three a larger one in proportion; and so on, with the curve rising steeply until the ownership of, say, a dozen in the territory over which the Government has power becomes economically impossible.

The chain shop, as we now know it, has, by the way, not only the evil of destroying the small distributor, but the further evil of controlling wholesale distribution and even production.

Suppose, for instance, a system of chain shops acting as fishmongers; a particular group extends until it controls the fishmongering business of, say, half the trade – say, for the sake of precision, 10,000 shops. It has not only destroyed the economic independence of 10,000 men who would have been each the free owner of a fishmonger's business; it has not only substituted for them 10,000 wage slaves liable to ruin at any moment by the arbitrary decision of an impersonal master who has no human relationship with them, but it is also in a position to dictate prices to the people who send the fish inland from the ports, and to control in great measure the nature and direction of the fisheries. That is manifestly a usurpation of social power and should be destroyed.

(2) The multiple shop also must be handicapped by differential taxation, based upon the number of categories with which it deals. One multiple shop (or department store) combines, let us say, in a particular case, fifty categories; it acts not only as a chemist and a boot-seller, a wine merchant and tobacconist, but as a stationer etc. Another deals with seventy categories, another with only twenty five. We need a tax differentiated by the number of categories. It will be easy for a small man to add some little extra activity to his main one – he can sell newspapers as well as tobacco, for instance – but when it comes to dealing with more than quite a few categories, differential taxation should begin, and before it came to dealing with the great number now occupying the chief department stores it should have become prohibitive.

It will be objected, of course, that for such a system you would need an extension of bureaucracy, that the definition of the various categories will be difficult etc. It is true that in all these reforms we shall have to extend, for the moment, bureaucratic action. The nature of the modern world is such that we cannot escape from being at least helped by the State in our reforms.

But in practice the danger is not so great as it seems, for the various forms of retail distribution are fairly well-established; there are divisions apparent to ordinary common sense, and this is so true that many of them, as it is, can only come into existence through a licence granted by, or purchased from, the State – tobacconists, for instance. Let that system be extended to a consider number of trades, and the thing is done.

There are licences for carrying on a tobacconist's shop and for carrying on a wine shop – let there be also a licence for carrying on a grocery and fishmongering business, or what not; let the licence be granted as a matter of right to any applicant; let its cost be insignificant to the man who applies for only one or two licences, but then let it begin to rise more and more steeply as the number of licences applied for increases.

(3) The third form of tax is a tax upon turnover. Your large retail distributor who has only one place of business, and who deals with only one kind of business can be, and is, in his way, destructive to the small man just as much as the large distributor who owns chains shops or as a multiple department store. Let there be no tax on turnover up to a certain sufficiently high level, then let it begin and grow steeply until it becomes prohibitive.

As to the second, converse, half of this policy. The money raised by the differential tax against large distribution, the money provided by that middle zone between the beginning of large distribution and the point where the differential tax becomes prohibitive, should be used to protect artificially the small man against the great. It should be used to establish and conserve corporate credit with the Guild to which – as we shall describe in a later article – the small distributor should belong; it should even be used, perhaps exceptionally, to subsidize the starting of the small man.

Here it may be objected that in many cases nowadays these reforms would be of no productive effect because the small distributor whom we are trying to save and to increase in number, is already a distributor only in name and has already become in practice a servant. This is notably the case with the tobacconists. The wholesale producer and distributor has made of the retail tobacconist nothing more than his agent; he can threaten the small retailer with extinction unless he buys at a dictated price and sells at a dictated price. The capitalist tyranny acts here as it does in the refreshment trade, with the "tied house." The remedy for this is a separate matter which we will deal with later on when we consider the reforms necessary in the control of production and wholesale distribution, but for the moment let the suggested reforms in the matter of retail distribution stand.

The opportunity for restoring the individual artisan and small human employer of craftsmen is, as has been said, far less than that for restoring the small distributor. For this there are two reasons. In the first place, concentrated production under large groups of capital can produce in many categories not *somewhat* cheaper than the individual or the small group, but *enormously* cheaper – though note that this is not universally true. Next (and this is really more important) fashion and habit have come in to help the evil. The purchaser has lost the habit of, and the desire for, choice.

I say that this spiritual disease is more important than the merely mechanical fact of cheap production. Such a statement will sound fantastic in the ears of those who are accustomed, as all modern men are, to implied materialism. Yet here, as in every other department, it is the mind that governs and not the material conditions. To see how true this is, consider what the effect actually is of choice exercised before our eyes in the modern world and what the effect would be if the use of choice were widely extended.

It is notorious that in certain districts, in certain trades covering great numbers of people, choice is still exercised and has a great effect. For an instance, I would quote the demand for Cheshire cheese among the Lancashire operatives. They know what they want and they insist upon it; they will not accept a substitute or an inferior article. See also the effect of choice as it is exercised (though in a restricted field, it is true), by the middle and upper middle classes in certain categories of furniture and design. Here, as in nearly everything else, the right process has been largely reversed; men take what is imposed upon them and not what they themselves choose. Supply controls demand and not demand supply. But there is still a sufficient amount of choice remaining, as anyone in the furniture trade will tell you, to produce considerable effect in the more expensive lines. Whether it be possible to effect such a moral revolution as reviving the general habit of choice only experiment can show. It has been done in some categories; in others it has quite failed. But in most it has not even been tried. With the exercise of choice, of individual will, of preferring this to that and seeing that you get it, you extend the opportunity for the artisan, the individual craftsman, the man who makes a thing to order, as also for the small master, the man who employs and personally supervises a few.

It must be admitted that there is only a limited field here available for the restoration of economic independence. Concentrated mechanical production will for long necessarily occupy the greater part of the economic area involved in any particular form of manufacture. Still, for the purpose of spreading the moral effect of economic independence, and familiarizing modern men with the idea thereof, the re-erection even of a small number of craftsmen *protected by a charter and guild* in some of our departments of production would be of the highest value.

Take, for example, the man who makes simple or more ornate wooden furniture on a small scale with personal knowledge of the methods, and without having recourse to concentrated mechanical means. We cannot replace him in his old position of making all the furniture needed in the community; he will, for a long time to come, account for no more than a small fraction; but we can easily multiply his present numbers by five, even by ten, perhaps by more than ten, and so set an example of what is desirable in the commonwealth. What is more, we could put before the eyes of people now unaccustomed to them objects of a proper shape, not turned out on a hideous pattern, which some capitalist group happens to find the cheapest, but suited to the tastes of the producer and the purchaser.

It must be admitted, of course, that in the beginning an effort of this kind would be the merest nibbling at the edges of a vast field. To our socialist opponents the effort will seem at first not only negligible, but ridiculous. We shall probably have a great deal less effect at first than had William Morris[7] and his school – for these, though at heart in favour of economic freedom, called themselves Socialists and were therefore listened to with some respect by people who had forgotten what property was. But if we could add to the moral effect a definite political weapon – the subsidizing and protecting of the small artisan at the expense of Big Business; the confirmation of the small artisan's position by a legalized Guild System (which I touch on in the latter part of this booklet) – we shall be able to do more than the dilettantes of the nineteenth century were ever able to effect, though in their time there was a much larger proportion of independent artisans remaining who might still have been saved.

In the case, therefore, of the artisan, as in the parallel case of the shop, the thing to work for is a revolution in political principle; a new set of ideas and therefore a new set of enactments, the reverse of those which built up industrial capitalism. We need enforceable laws and actual institutions which shall artificially advantage the small distributor against the great, and the small craftsman or small user of machinery against the large manufacturer. That is, of course, "uneconomic." In other words, it will cost effort. So do the luxuries personally enjoyed by the big capitalists today. A well-made piece of furniture, neither repulsive nor mechanical in design, will cost more than a piece turned out by mass production. But you are buying something for society at that price, and it is a something well worth society's while – much better worth while in our eyes than cheap furniture. That "something" is citizenship, and the escape from slavery.

I am here tempted to repeat the objection that must occur to the reader throughout this essay: "All this is moonshine, because there is no condition of mind in a modern industrial State prepared for such a political change." Possibly not. But at any rate those are lines, and the only lines, along which the change can be effected. The small distributor and the small craft producer could thus be re-established. He would not be made universal; he would at first be only a rather larger minority than the present small minority is; but he would from the first be more secure than he is at present, though he would not at first appear in the community in very much larger numbers. Also those numbers would grow.

But, apart from his numbers, the mere presence of the secure small owner, after we *had* made him secure, would have remedial effect. His presence would be an object lesson in freedom and establishment, and let us hope, a hint to his neighbours to change their own condition, where this was possible, from one of wage slavery to one of independence.

Even were such a policy successful beyond any limits now thought possible, there must remain a very large field in which the individual craftsman or the small human employer of craftsmen, the individual small shopkeeping family has no place. Vast areas of modern production and exchange will necessarily concern great units and great units alone. How shall these be dealt with? How shall well-divided property re-arise in those fields of economic effort where the small unit can in the nature of modern things have no place?

That is the next question to be answered, and I shall now deal with it. After that I shall ask how a similar policy can be applied to the land; in the last section I shall deal with the political organization necessary for consolidating the position of small property by guild and charter, and corporate credit when it shall have been restored.

IV

I SAID AT THE END OF MY LAST DIVISION THAT, after the comparatively straightforward task of restoring *in some degree* (but as much as possible) the small distributor, and in a necessarily lesser degree (but as much as possible) the craftsman, we should have to tackle a more serious task, the distribution of ownership in those great units of production, distribution, transport, etc, which cannot of their nature be worked "severally" as can the forge, the carpenter's shop or the grocery. These large units cover nearly all the field in the highly industrialized countries such as England, but they cover a large part of it in nearly all powerful modern nations, and an appreciable part even in those which can still be called agricultural.

This field of the large unit has tended to become larger and larger in the last lifetime and is still expanding. The economic area in which you cannot hope to recreate the small distributor and the small craftsman has tended to increase at the expense of the area in which you can restore him.

This tendency is due to two quite different causes, between which it is most important to distinguish, especially as most of those who deal with these matters in our modern economic writing confuse them badly. There is, first of all:—

(a) The economic unit which has, *from the nature of the instrument used*, to be worked on a large scale; the classical example is the railway system.

Next you have:—

(b) The economic unit which becomes a large one, not from the nature of things, not because the instruments used must be gathered together in one centre or under one combination and control, but because the elimination of competitive costs, and even the greater perfection of methods accompanying amalgamation, tend to produce such great units. Here the force at work is not a mechanical one. It is the character of men and has nothing to do with the nature of the instruments concerned – or little to do with it – and much more to do with the effects of untrammelled competition.

We have seen how true this is of the chain shop and the big store, and the same thing is at work, of course, in production and transport. You see it in the eating up of the small motor bus services by new big combines, which should logically grow into one great "combine"; you see it in the production of such things as gramophone records in great centralized factories, and in many such factories under one control – and, of course, in scores of other instances.

I say it is all-important to distinguish between the two kinds of tendency: they are to be dealt with in quite different fashions. The defenders of industrial capitalism – such few of them as are left – and those with the same type of mind who defend Socialism, and its only logical form, Communism, have told us over and over again that amalgamation is inevitable. They call it an "economic necessity" because they think that any instrument or method cheaper or more efficient for the special purpose of production or transport must necessarily oust the somewhat less cheap or somewhat less efficient. They also imply that there is a necessity for the greedier man and the more cunning man to eat up the more generous and less instructed.

They who talk thus confuse what they here call "necessity" with that true necessity imposed by universal physical laws independent of the human will. There is no *necessity* for amalgamation into larger and larger units, where the instruments used do not of themselves impose larger and larger units. The only "necessity" here is the logical necessity of consequences following upon certain human arrangements. Where you have arranged the rules of the game in any particular fashion, there will necessarily follow certain consequences, but those consequences no longer follow when you change the rules of the game.

If you were to declare immunity for those who stole watches there would follow as a necessity a great deal of watch-stealing as compared with the stealing of other objects. If there were no punishment for assault you would find weaker men, physically, bullied all over the place by stronger men; and in the same way if there is no restriction of competition or of the scale of ownership or of the size of amalgamation and control thereof, then, indeed, there is a sort of necessity making for the increase of the economic unit. But it is only "necessity" so long as the rules stand thus – change the rules and the necessity disappears.

Where, however, the instrument used is of such a nature that it can only be used on a large scale then there is indeed a necessity for a large economic unit. I have quoted the railways as the classical example of this. To build a railway from Bilbao to Leon[8] will cost a very large sum indeed; you will have to prepare the gradients, to build bridges, make cuttings, pierce tunnels through the mountains, and when you have done all that you must have your rolling stock and the rest – you cannot operate the thing save as one very large unit. But there is no *necessity* that all motor buses going along an already existing road from Bilbao to Leon should be owned by one big combine, or one rich person, or even all controlled from one centre. They will only tend to be so controlled if you leave competition unchecked; that is if your society and your laws are so organized that property is safeguarded by the laws while its good distribution is not safeguarded.

Now our policy in dealing with these two quite distinct groups of large units should, I think, be four fold:—

1. In the matter of units which are *necessarily* large, because the large instrument alone is capable of doing the work, we

must watch every opportunity of substituting the smaller unit for the larger whenever a new discovery permits this; but where there is no such opportunity, where the large unit is inevitable, we must have control either for the purpose of creating well-distributed property in the shares thereof, or for the purpose of managing the use of it as a communal concern. For instance, much of the centralized mechanical production of our time arose when expensive and necessarily centralized steam power supplanted man power. It now could be decentralized through the widely distributed use of electrical power. A differential tax on power used would effect this. Use a differential tax to make the electrical power cheaper per unit when used on a small scale by the small man than when used on a large scale.

2. Where amalgamation and the formation of large units is due not to the nature of the instrument but to unchecked competition, we must deliberately reverse the process, as in the case of the shopkeeper and craftsman. We must penalize amalgamation and support division of units. For instance, the grinding of wheat into flour has become the monopoly of a few large mills which took advantage of the Great War. It would be immediately possible to penalize these by differential taxation and restore the smaller millers by the subsidy thus available.

3. In all cases where separately owned shares in the unit are possible (and they are nearly always possible) we should aim at creating the largest possible number of shareholders and at preventing the growth of large blocks of shares under one control.

4. We should especially act against that typical modern evil which may be called "irresponsible control," whereby the economic unit is managed without real responsibility to the shareholders, and even without the real possession of the shares by those who control them.

Let us take these four points one by one.

1. The process of discovery and application does not (as was arbitrarily affirmed in the nineteenth century and even later)

necessarily make for the large unit. New discoveries and new applications do not produce in any inevitable way the expensive instrument as against the inexpensive. The idea that they do so was, like most so-called "scientific" ideas, an irrational conclusion drawn from blind habitual experience, which did not consider the logical nature of the problem

It was the experience of those who began the use of modern machinery that the machines to their hand grew increasingly expensive as they grew more efficient and could be used very much better – often could only be used – in large centralized fashion. The system was already well started and had gathered momentum when new instruments appeared eminently favourable for a smaller division of the unit. But the opportunity was not fully taken advantage of precisely because of that momentum gained by the earlier system of large units. First we had the electric motor, whereby power could be almost infinitely divided; next we had the internal combusion engine whereby it could be still further divided, especially for the purposes of transport. Of this somewhat more advantage was taken than of electricity; but in both cases the advantage was rapidly neutralized by amalgamations which had nothing to do with the nature of the instrument but were merely the result of uncontrolled competition and political corruption; the rich man swallowing up the poor man and bringing "pressure" to bear for the passing of regulations hampering his humbler rival. What that word "pressure" means in all its forms of bribery and blackmail, every political assembly knows.

What the future may reserve for us in the way of new instruments we cannot tell, but at any rate with those already in hand there is an indefinitely large field for the expansion of well-divided membership.

In those cases where the instrument is necessarily very expensive we may, as I have said, adopt one of two methods: we may either promote the ownership of it into shares, the proper division of which and the saving of which from irresponsible control will be later discussed; or we may accept the principle of communal ownership, whether by a Guild or by the State, but under the general proviso that ownership by the State is better avoided where possible, because the private citizen has no control over the State as he has over the Guild.

State ownership is better, of course, than ownership by a few very rich individuals, or even the ownership by many small shareholders who are at the mercy of a few rich ones, as they are under our English company law, but there is always the danger in State ownership that the men who work for the State-owned instrument will turn, if they are not turned already, into wage slaves, without other support than the weekly provision made for them by their master – the State.

This is not strictly and necessarily the result, but it tends to be the result. The Belgian and Italian railway systems, for instance, the one when it was State-owned, and the other still being State-owned, worked, and work very well for the community and remained curiously free from the corruption which so-called "representative institutions" always breed. The Parliamentarians of the two States in question left, I understand, a clean working and efficient bureaucracy to do the management, though no doubt they occasionally put themselves and their hangers-on into particular jobs connected with the monopoly. We must not start with the principle that State *ownership* is always bad through its tendency both to inefficiency and corruption; but we *must* start with the proviso that it should be avoided wherever possible, in cases of active exploitation, although State *protection* by charter for the purpose of preventing irresponsible monopoly is essential. A chartered guild composed of the workers in the system would be one form of communal system securing a better distribution of wealth; so would a chartered shareholding company, to which the rules we are about to consider (applicable to all shareholding and designed with the object of a good division of property in the shares) should apply.

But in all this department we must remember that the necessarily large unit covers a far smaller field than is generally imagined. There is the railway; there is the Post Office, including telephones and telegraphs; there is the road system of the country. But the great mass of production, distribution and transport does not fall under this category. It is not monopolist of necessity. It only becomes so by bad human arrangements which can be bettered.

Meanwhile every new discovery or new application of an existing discovery, which makes for the break-up of monopoly must be fostered. For instance, it is directly against our policy to bolster up the railway against well-divided road transport. It is, on the contrary, part of our policy to favour the new road transport against the railway, because road transport can be worked in small units and the railways cannot.

But it is essential that our support of rural transport should be a support of the small man and that we should differentiate strongly against the use of the road by the great units, especially those which deal in heavy goods. Railway property has at least become better distributed than most of the great capitalist groups, whereas some of the monopolies which are getting the advantage of road transport at the public charge are virtually in the hands of half a dozen men and often – as in the case of oils – the property of aliens.

2. As to those amalgamations into large units which are the result of competition and human arrangements independent of the nature of the instrument used, we can act there exactly as it was proposed to act in the matter of the chain shop. We can penalize the large unit, and subsidize and advantage in every way the smaller unit.

This does not mean, of course, that we can break up units which of their nature must be of a certain size. One type of production will need an organization such that you cannot have less than a certain size of unit connected with it, another will require a still larger size, and in every such case you will, for the better distribution of property, have to organize for property in the form of shareholding. But what is essential is to prevent the amalgamation of units beyond the maximum size required for actual production in that particular department.

For instance, you may say: "We cannot make incandescent lamps in the modern fashion without such and such a minimum amount of capital. It is necessary for the making of the lamps that such considerable units should exist." Yes, but it is not necessary that many factories should be amalgamated into one. Production and distribution may be rendered somewhat cheaper by so doing, the work may even be somewhat more efficiently done, but the price you have to pay in the loss of freedom is a great deal too high.

Another striking example is breweries. Today they tend to be few and centralized. Better beer and a greater choice would result from penalizing the large brewery and with the revenue subsidizing the small one, down to the cottage brewer.

In the mixed cases you must advantage the smaller unit against the greater. An excellent example is the modern production of footgear. Footgear can be produced by machinery on a large scale, and much more cheaply than it can be by the hand craftsman. Such footgear is also much worse than that produced by the hand craftsman. But you cannot, with modern urban populations, abandon the mechanical production of footgear. What could be done would be to encourage the hand craftsman so that his necessarily small numbers should at any rate be extended as much as possible. You should tax the mechanical production, and, above all, you should see to it that there should be no amalgamation of factories or establishment of very large factories, where, at no very considerable loss of efficiency, the smaller factory will do.

In other words, you must here, as everywhere, reverse the present current economic life; you must do the opposite of what was done by those who began the industrialization of the modern world – you must act in a fashion which *they* would have called reactionary. *That spirit of reaction must run through all our effort at the restoration of property if there is to be any chance of its even partial success.*

3. The setting up of smaller units held in shares and controlled by Guild or company monopolies, where these are necessary, will be of no service to those who desire to restore property unless the shares are well distributed.

To effect a good distribution therein you must apply differential taxation, in three ways:–

First, to the size of the individual shareholding group. You must make it difficult for the large group to buy up the smaller one. You must make it easy for the smaller group to start at the expense of the larger one, and then to grow to a certain size in spite of the efforts the larger one will make to crush it.

Secondly, you must limit the individual holding of shares; not by arbitrary legislation (merely saying that not more than so many shares may be held in one hand), but again, by differential taxation. Where the holder of so many shares desires to increase his holding he must pay a tax which rises so steeply that as his accumulation proceeds it is soon checked, and the proceeds of that tax can be put to subsidizing of purchase by the smaller holders. That is a new principle to which we are quite unaccustomed, but without it the restoration of property will not begin.

Thirdly, there must be a capital tax on industrial shares (as distinguished from land, which is in a different category altogether). More must be provided by such a capital tax and less by income tax. Thus only do you really differentiate against the big holder.

It may be argued that we have something of the kind already in the Death Duties. To this argument, I answer that the parallel is false. The Death Duties do not prevent accumulation nor redistribute it after it is made; all they do is to take away a certain part of private accumulation and dissipate it in keeping alive various State functionaries, and paying usury (principally to the banks) on non-productive State debts. But a capital tax on the value of shares held, and levied continuously on the amount held, would automatically produce the desired result.

When you have these forces at work in combination a wide distribution of ownership of shares will necessarily follow.

4. Lastly, we must provide against that worst of modern evils in matters of shareholding – irresponsible control. As things are today you get the following state of affairs:—

Some swindler (to give his true name) having 51% of the shares in a company (we will call it A) puts forward company A as the purchaser of 51% of the shares in Company B. In other words, he uses the property of the other 49% of the shareholders in Company A, without responsibility to them, and makes Company A the controller of Company B. He then uses his control of Company B to purchase 51% of the shares of Company C – and so on. At last one individual (or small group) has in his hands the control of an indefinitely large number of shareholders to whom he is not responsible.

The actual process has, of course, become by this time infinitely more complicated than that and is capable of any amount of modification, but that is the principle at work.

In order to defeat it there must be an established principle that:—

(a) There shall be no majority control save through a very large majority, certainly more than 51% and better 90%. A small proportion of individual share*holders* (not of share *value*) should suffice to veto a policy or change.

(b) No affiliation of companies, nor power of purchase of shares by a company as a person.

Now we remark that irresponsible control is also called "inevitable" through the breakdown of an unwieldy machinery of voting. A general meeting of shareholders is really no control at all. It was designed for a time when all society was differently organized, smaller and much simpler. There is no reason why voting power in shareholders should be unwieldy were the companies reasonably small, and there is no reason why voting on all major proposals should not be done by post. Here comes in the difficulty, as there must come in all these things, the question of degree. Which proposals are so important that the opinion of the shareholders must be taken? With a good distribution of property and a habit of well distributed shareholding, and a growth of small units, common sense would soon decide this on its largest lines.

Take a case of which the lines in the main (as I remember them) were these: Some years ago a company with a very large number of shareholders was got hold of by an "operator" (to use the euphemism he himself affected). It was a company owning many hotels. He "controlled" it, if I remember right, by the method which I have given in simplified form above. He did not personally own the bulk of the hotel property. He even indirectly controlled but a very small fraction of it. But his control over the whole was nonetheless absolute. His own business in life happened to be the sale of furniture – whether it was his direct business as a manufacturer, or whether he had got it through yet another series of operations, I forget. At any rate, he started to make the hotels in question furnish themselves completely to his advantage – to purchase furniture they did not need at a higher price than they should have paid – in order to fill his own pockets as a seller of furniture. In that case the thing was exposed and widely talked about because the "operator" made some technical mistake or other which enabled his victims to bring him into court. But it is a model of the kind of thing flourishing on all sides in a thousand different forms. If it proceeds unchecked it makes the good distribution and security of shareholding impossible.

To all these propositions it will be replied, of course, as in the former examples, that they are impracticable. The whole structure of the modern world renders this so. The evil of Industrial Capitalism is now mature; it has taken firm root; it has developed and is now "set" in all its complications. You could not undo even a part of it without a crash – even if you had despotic power; and to hope to do so without despotic power is plainly chimerical. You would never get opinion to move – for opinion has been formed in the very atmosphere of that which you are trying to destroy.

To this I answer, first, that our effort at restoring property does not aim at perfection nor even at any large universal upheaval of the existing system. It aims at making a beginning. Just as in the case of the craftsman we know that we cannot put him back where he was before ugly and imperfect things, turned out mechanically, began to oust his much better forms of production. Just as we cannot hope to see in our time the great stores disappear and the lesser and much more useful shopkeepers take their place; just as we cannot even hope probably for any very large curtailment, at any rate for some considerable time, of the pernicious multiple shop system, so we cannot quickly and on a large scale remedy share-shuffling. But, as in the case both of the distributor and the craftsman, we can make a beginning. We can plant a seed and we may doubtfully hope that this seed will grow.

Such should be our aims in the matters of shareholding in industrial concerns, in the size of the units and the curtailment of irresponsible control of them.

And I would add that in the whole process a very powerful factor making for success would be the public knowledge of how much is held and by whom, and a continued attack upon that secrecy which is half the evil of the present state of affairs.

Secondly, I would answer, what I fear may seem paradoxical (I have already said it on a past page), that the effort to be made not only does not attempt completion, not only will be satisfied with beginnings, but will very probably fail, even in such a very limited field. The forces against even the partial success of such an attempt are ubiquitous and highly organized, and what is worse, they have become instinctive. Capitalism and its Socialist fruit are taken for granted today in England as the natural air of the country.

The reaction towards health will not be easy, even on a small scale, but, once more, the excuse for attempting it is that the alternative is clear. Either we restore property or we restore slavery, to which we have already gone more than halfway in our industrialized society. I do not discuss here whether slavery (whether to a very rich man, or group of men, or to the State) is a bad thing, or a good thing. I only say that, without well distributed property, freedom cannot be; and that, if we leave things as they are, slavery must come.

There are many who will say that shareholding in large concerns, however well distributed, is a most imperfect way of realizing economic freedom. True and full economic freedom is only present when a man himself possesses and himself uses the instruments of his craft. The carpenter who makes a table with his own tools exercises a very different function from the same carpenter who happens also to hold shares in a railway, debentures, bonds in national and municipal debts, and so forth. As a craftsman at work he is in full control, personal and alive; as a shareholder his control is distant, indirect and largely impersonal.

The criticism is profoundly just. The structure of modern share and bond holding was built up in an atmosphere hostile to full economic freedom and its fruits are not in harmony with such freedom.

But a policy of emancipation must deal with things as they are. The carpenter with £30 a year from public bonds (the average family share if an exact distribution existed) with another £30 say, from debentures and shares, is in a much more independent position than the same carpenter dependent upon his craft alone, in a society where the cream of social production is skimmed off for the benefit of a plutocratic class. He has reserves.

V

HE RESTORATION OF PROPERTY MEANS, AND HAS meant throughout history in nearly all places and times, primarily, the restoration of property in *land*.

When men have become wage slaves they think in terms of income. When they are economically free they think in terms of property. Most modern men living under industrial conditions regard economic reform as essentially a redistribution of income; property is for them an illusion; the reality behind it is income. Property for them means only an arrangement whereby a certain income is secured. Free men look at it just the other way. They think of income as the product of property; and the typical form of property, which is also the foundational form, is property in *land*. Under the eastern despotisms, as also under barbaric, nomad conditions, property in land is either denied in theory or unknown in practice, but in our Western world it is, and has been throughout all our development, the guarantee of citizenship and the foundation thereof.

Of this account there is throughout the West (that is, throughout Christendom) an instinct for preserving or, if it has been lost, for restoring widely distributed property in land. During all the stable periods in our civilization such a wide distribution of property in land, among free men at any rate, was the rule. When it became the exception society grew troubled; and that unnatural state of affairs – the presence of men politically free but economically unfree – produced dangerous strains resulting sometimes in a violent transformation of society.

That is what happened in the heart of the Roman Empire towards the end of its highest period. During the Dark Ages well distributed property in land gradually reappeared. During the Middle Ages it was the universal rule. Even in the early part thereof the serf might still be constrained to work for his Lord, but he was secure in the ownership of a portion of his native land not subject to competitive rent, inalienable so long as the customary dues were paid; and his land passed on from him to his descendants. In most countries this state of affairs developed after the Middle Ages into the establishment of a free peasantry, that is, of citizens possessing, in numbers sufficient to determine the character of their society, land of their own, coupled with political as well as economic freedom.

There were parts of Europe, however, in which the clock was set back, notably in Great Britain. The peasantry were swallowed up by the greater land owners and became a proletariat. In this country the historical process is now familiar to many – perhaps by this time to most educated men, though our official academic history long remained silent upon it. First came the strengthening of the greater land owners by the loot of the Church in the sixteenth century, then in the seventeenth century came the eating up by the greater land owners of the smaller yeomanry, notably under that ironically entitled Statute of Frauds, passed, as has been repeated in these pages, by Parliament, that is, by the greater land owners themselves (who were by that time masters of the country) in the reign of Charles II.[9] Today England is the typical example of a country in which the desire for land and the sense of ownership in it has, for the mass of the people, fallen to its lowest.

English conditions therefore afford the "zero point" for a policy of recovery. If it be possible to restore well distributed property in land under English conditions today, it will be possible to restore such well distributed property in land anywhere.

Here, however, we must repeat the principle laid down at the beginning of this essay, that you will not get well distributed property in any form, whether in land or anything else, unless there is some desire present in the community for its acquirement. There must be some spark left in the embers if you are to coax them again into flame; you cannot compel people to become economically free if they do not desire economic freedom at all: if they have so completely lost the instinct for it that they confuse the reception of a secure revenue with freedom. A secure revenue can be guaranteed under any form of slavery – State slavery or private slavery. Such security is not only not identical with, but, as an ideal, actually militates against, economic freedom.

Now at this point we must introduce very important distinctions, too often left on one side. These distinctions are as follows:—

(1) A distinction between agricultural and urban land, or, to make a more exact definition, a distinction between land mainly occupied for the production of agricultural stuff and land occupied by the man who produces things by machinery or as a craftsman.

(2) A distinction between land occupied by the owner and land occupied by someone other than the owner, who pays a rent for it to that other. And let us remember that in all this discussion the word "land" includes buildings and other immovables attached to land.

It must be a first principle in attempting the reconstruction of property in land that agricultural land shall be treated differently from urban land, and that the burden upon land occupied by the owner shall be markedly less than the burden upon land and used as a source of profit by letting it out to others. Both these distinctions are revolutionary as applied to the society in which we live today. Both are essential to the recovery of property in land.

As to the second, the distinction between land used by the owner and land not used by him, unless it is made and insisted upon and expressed in social law and custom, the effort at the reconstruction of well distributed property in land fails. Today a man in England inheriting from his father a house to which the rental value is, say, £100 a year, is taxed upon it exactly as though he was getting £100 a year rent by letting it out to somebody else. This social falsehood is fundamental, and undermines the whole situation. There must be a radical difference in the burdens imposed upon land occupied, as land (according to our view) should be occupied, by a human family living thereon, and land occupied by others from whom the owner draws tribute. Throughout the history of our civilization the pretence that the two were the same has led to the breakdown of society, and if we desire to restore society we must restore the simple principle that a man living under his own roof, and on his own land, shall have the advantage over a man who uses his property only to exploit others.

But as to distinguishing between agricultural and urban land, or let us say between land occupied mainly for agricultural production, and the house with or without a garden occupied by a craftsman, or even by the wage slave, the problem is different because under modern conditions there is difficulty in separating the two.

You can settle simply enough by inquisition and declaration whether a man is or is not paying rent to others for the privilege of a human home, but it is not so easy to distinguish nowadays between land that is urban and land that is rural.

In the thirteenth century the distinction was clear, and it is clearer today in societies where there is a strong peasantry than in societies based upon industrialism. Even in England it is possible to draw a working distinction. Land can be registered and by inspection verified as used in the main for one purpose or for the other, with the policy of always leaning towards the recognition of the agricultural rather than the urban type, that is, the policy of calling a piece of land in doubtful cases agricultural rather than urban.

As for the urban type, there ought to be a simple rule: every lease should automatically contain the power of purchase by installment; any lease not containing such a clause should be void if it were a lease for more than a certain number of years. And, should this ordinance lead to the restriction of long leases, that should be met by forbidding the short lease without the option of renewal for a longer period.

It will be argued, of course, that the greater part of tenancy under the industrial system today cannot envisage ultimate proprietorship: the wage slaves are too nomadic and too thoroughly dispossessed for that. But such an objection misconceives our object. We are not attempting to reconstruct property in land universally and at short notice. We are attempting a beginning wherever conditions may be favourable. And if today these conditions were observed with regard even to urban land a beginning could be made.

Now, as to agricultural land, which is the real crux of the affair, even in such countries as ours (I mean England, Scotland and Wales, excluding Ireland) the problem has a special character of its own.

Let us suppose that there be in Great Britain today (England, Scotland and Wales) a sufficient remnant of men with the tradition of using the land. What are the conditions under which this remnant may be fostered and made to grow? If we can be certain of these, in the island as it now is, we can *a fortiori* apply those principles to other countries where the desire for land is more widely spread.

There would seem to apply to this problem the following principles, which I do not put down in any order of importance, for each of them is essential.

(1) You cannot make a peasant direct out of a townsman. You may graft the townsman onto the peasant; an existing peasantry can train and teach and digest into itself a certain moderate proportion of townsmen, but you cannot take the townsman and set him down on the land, even under the most favourable conditions, and expect him to live upon it. He will

fail (as the phrase goes) "to make a living"; that is, he will soon throw up his job in disgust.

You will get exceptional men here and there who can transform themselves. There are still men in the towns who have hereditary instincts for the land; there are others who develop even without experience an understanding of the land. But the mass of men brought up under urban conditions, come on the thing the wrong way round, and are therefore soon repelled by it. They are often attracted by the externals of country life, but have no inkling for its inward practice. Their conception and, what is more important, their habit of labour is mechanical repetition through a limited number of hours during which they have to work at a pressure which renders such limitation necessary.

Agricultural work is the other way about. It is multiple rather than repetitive. It is not generally intense. It cannot be limited in hours, but must be indefinitely elastic. Further, there is this fundamental spiritual difference between the two: agricultural work is an interest when it is pursued for its own sake, while modern mechanical work is a grievous task of which men always desire to be rid as soon as may be. The peasant goes on working slowly in his highly varied task throughout the whole of a long summer's day, and is filled with his occupation. But he keeps it voluntary, prepared to take his own recreation at his own times and to fill in with this or that the hours when he cannot work in the open.

(2) The second principle is this: The land will supply under well divided property no more than a modest sustenance under normal conditions. The man with a small freehold which he cultivates himself with the aid of his family must not expect to be better off and usually will not be so well off, reckoning in cash values, as the wage slave of a corresponding station in society.

It is one of the first things remarked by a wage slave coming from industrial societies to live among a peasantry that the peasants are "beggarly." There is, of course, another reason for this besides the fact that the land must not be expected to provide more than a moderate sustenance, that other reason being the passion of the peasant for independence. It makes him keen to grasp at the smallest sums of money, to hesitate on spending where he can save, to abhor magnificence, luxuries, and every form of what he feels to be waste.

I have used the phrase, "in cash values," but to this there is an important reservation. Cobbett's[10] small freeholder with a pig, perhaps a couple of milch cows, and communal rights over and above his limited pasturage and arable, would not, if you added up the market value of all that he got by his labour, have an income superior to the regularly paid labourer of the town. But he has two advantages: freedom, that is, a sustenance under his own control; and quality, that is a sustenance better in every way, in material, in hours, in choice, in *locale*. The peasant eats not only of his own produce but off his own table and at his own hours; and he eats better food and brews better drink.

(3) The third principle attaching to well divided property in agricultural land is the principle that a man should himself live off the actual produce as much as possible. That, in practice, he can hardly ever do so altogether, is true; there will always be division of labour, and with a peasantry determined on acquiring a maximum in order to preserve its independence, such differentiation will often be pushed to an extreme limit. You will find many cases upon the Continent of men who live upon a tiny patch of vineyard. Their direct sustenance therefrom is only, say, a couple of gallons of wine a week for themselves and their dependents. They must obtain their bread and meat and clothing and necessary repairs of house and steading from the sale of their surplus. If the wine is of a special quality they will not even drink of their own produce but sell it all. Even where there is a mixed holding much will be sold under the conditions of a high civilization for the purchase of necessaries which the holding does not provide. But the underlying principle remains, and the more it is kept in view the sounder will the position be: "Live of your own."

(4) The fourth principle will, I am afraid, when it is stated plainly, appear fantastic, but it is essential. The burden laid upon the land of the small owner must be light, the tribute he has to pay – wherein I include usury in all its forms – must be a minimum. In other words, when you are attempting to re-establish a peasantry under adverse conditions, that peasantry must be *privileged* as against the diseased society around it.

Today false statistics could easily be prepared showing that a great mass of English land is in the possession of those who till it; but as a fact it is really in the possession of money lenders – principally the banks. The ownership is nominal; the real control is in the money lending power which exacts tribute. Now, unless you are prepared to start afresh with a system under which usury shall not drain the lifeblood of the tiller of the soil, your efforts will fail. Even co-operative banks, of which we will speak later, should play a subsidiary, not a dominating part. The tillage of the land on a small scale is such that if you burden it with these outgoings of usury you wound it with a wound which will ultimately bleed it to death. And what is true of usury is equally true of every other form of tribute.

I have in mind, as I write, one patch of land, a concrete case, of which I know all the details: thirty acres of land of an average quality in a purely agricultural district. The true burden of taxation weighing upon this small farm is, as things now are, to begin with, an income tax upon the rental; although no rent be paid, although the land and the house upon it be in the possession of the tiller. This income tax, being graduated, may in the case of the small owner be small; but it exists. In the particular case I am considering, as the 30 acres belong to an owner of other wealth, the Income Tax is about £4.10s.3p an acre. The tithe, which is I admit a heavy one, comes to nearly six shillings an acre. The land is already to some extent subsidized by the abolition of agricultural rates, but there is the rate upon the house, a rate of four shillings in the pound upon the supposed rental value. I do not speak of the burden of upkeep in gates and the rest which a certain social standard imposes and which, were a free peasantry in existence, would be greatly lowered at the expense of what are now called "good appearances." The mere money burden of the rates and taxes, including the tithe, is more than the thing will bear. The effect of them upon the small owner is just what it would be upon the urban worker if he were asked to pay £15 a year out of his subsistence wage. Quite apart from any question of usurious tribute it is a burden more than the thing will stand.

To these main principles there are two more which I would add: first the necessity of co-operation among the small owners for the purposes of marketing and for the lowering of the costs of production – for instance, co-operation in the dairy business. The second is the permission of alienation.

The reason I exclude these two from the main principles is because a peasantry once established will solve such problems for itself. Co-operation will naturally arise, and the restriction of absolute ownership by rules forbidding alienation kill effort: they are a form of servitude. A free peasantry once established will see to itself. Make it unfree by too close a supervision from any form of bureaucracy, and the moral motive power will be maimed.

There is further, a final principle which, while not essential, is operative for good and it lies immediately to our hand. It is the principle that everything should be done by the artifice of law to make it easy for the smaller man to buy land from the richer man, and difficult for the larger man to buy land from the smaller man. You must establish what is called upon the Continent a "cadastrum." There must be a register of land (it already exists in practice through the income tax schedules) and you must establish by a differential tax – the principle of which you can find in the Wyndham Land Act[11] in Ireland – a tendency for the small man to buy from the great, and for the great to sell to the small.

Granted such principles underlying your effort, applying that effort to men who are already tilling the land and have an hereditary faculty therein, leaving yourself free to feed into such a system new men hitherto unconnected with the land but capable of being grafted onto an existing peasantry, and your peasantry will prosper and grow. It will grow slowly. It will not, for a very long time become the predominant note in a society already morally ruined by industrialism. But it will form a nucleus of health in such a society.

It is evident from what has been said that any such attempt to re-erect a peasantry in a society where the idea of peasantry has almost disappeared must be based upon subsidy, that is, upon gift. You have to foster the new growth, and that can only be done at the expense of other forms of wealth surrounding the new growth. If in England, for instance, you abolish the tithe on the small man (keep it by all means upon the large man) someone will have to find the difference or you will be robbing the tithe owner. The same is true of taxes and of rates. In other words, you cannot start a new peasantry save at the expense of the diseased society surrounding it; and if you are not prepared to impose that sacrifice your peasantry will never be established. It *must* begin as a social luxury and, while it remains in that initial "luxury" state, it must like all luxuries be extravagantly paid for. What you have to decide is whether there is remaining among us enough tradition to start a peasantry again – the poor beginnings of one, the seedling – and, if so, whether it is worth while to the health and the morals of the community that the economic effort should be made.

I have said nothing in reply to those who maintain that a peasantry cannot now be restored because mechanical large scale agriculture must now necessarily destroy the small owner and cultivator. I have wasted no space on that kind of thing for two very good reasons: First that the presumption is as false here as in manufacture: machinery and large combinations do not exclude small property, which can always act in combination; second that we have all around us in the real world, as distinguished from academic writing, peasantries holding their own and surpassing the capitalist exploitation of the land.

VI

IGH TAXATION IS INCOMPATIBLE WITH THE GEN-
eral institution of property. The one kills the
other. Where property is well distributed resis-
tance to big taxation is so fierce and efficacious
that big taxation breaks down. Where an effort is being made
to restore well divided property, high taxation will destroy that
effect.

There is no need to delay upon a definition of what consti-
tutes high taxation as distinguished from normal taxation; like
everything in which there is a process of gradation, any definition can be quarrelled with, and every definition will depend
upon degree. But we know very well what the thing is. High
taxation is taxation which has passed the point after which it
becomes a continuous burden of anxiety and interference upon
the productive man.

John Stuart Mill ventured the judgement that 10% was a
fair rough limit to establish. When you took more than 10%
of a man's earnings, or even other income, you began to pass
the limit after which the thing interfered with and warped the
normal processes of economic life. But, in fact, no numeri-
cal standard can be exactly applied. Obviously 10% levied on a
man with £5,000 a year, living off State payment of interest, is
quite a different thing from 10% levied on a small shopkeeper
struggling to keep going with £200 a year profit. Ten percent
in direct taxation demanded at one moment in the year is altogether a different thing psychologically from 10% spread out in

indirect taxation upon a number of petty luxuries. We know very well in practice when high taxation is present and when it is not, and we know that since the Great War the nations of our own civilization, and particularly Great Britain, have had to endure taxation which has been, and remains, fantastically high.

That high taxation is the enemy of well distributed property is apparent in two ways. First, it is apparent in the fact that it can be levied effectively only in proportion as well distributed property has disappeared. Second, its effect in operation is to destroy the process whereby well distributed property is accumulated.

Very high taxation indeed – such confiscatory taxation as we are suffering in England today – is impossible where property is well distributed. You can have taxation somewhat too high indeed where property is well distributed, and it will do great harm to the institution of property and gradually impair its good distribution; but to have much higher taxation still working efficiently and producing its full amount, you need a society like our own in which small property has decayed.

The reason is simple: it may be put colloquially by saying that you can tax a man with £20,000 a year more heavily in proportion than you can tax a man with £2,000 a year. You can take away, annually, half the income of a very rich man and yet leave him very rich, but if you take away half that of a small man you ruin him. This plain arithmetical truth is observable again in the necessary presence of gradation whenever taxation becomes abnormal. When taxation is normal and low, not disturbing the economic life of the average citizen, you can have a flat rate above a certain very low minimum, and this is, as a fact, what we had in this country in the levying of the income tax before the quite recent and disastrous changes began. If we put on an income tax of 4d in the pound – less than 2% – we can, after exempting the very small incomes, levy it without friction and without injustice upon the rest of the community. Even a man with £200 a year is not seriously disturbed by having to pay less than £4; and though, under a flat rate, the greater the fortune the less the real burden imposed on it, yet the burden is everywhere so slight that no evil results accrue. When you come to high and oppressive taxation you are compelled as by a physical law to graduate. You have to make the burden much greater on the larger fortunes than on the smaller and on the larger incomes than on the smaller, otherwise you could not raise the tax at all. The consequence is that in a nation where much the greater part of the population are living on a wage or salary, and where huge accumulations (which have been well called the "negation of property") are the mark of society, very high taxation can be levied successfully and a much larger proportionate revenue produced than in a society of equal wealth where property is better distributed.*

The thing can be put diagrammatically. Suppose in a community in which the total surplus (that is, rents, usury and profits) comes to £2,000,000 a year, and that of this two million pounds one half – £1,000,000 – is divided among ten families while the other half is divided among ten thousand families; then the bulk of the community (the poorer people) have over and above their earnings £100 a year unearned income each. Suppose the average of earnings in the poorer part for each family is £100 a year – then the average total income for these poorer families will be £200 a year. You could not in practice take away one half from these small incomes by taxation. But you could take away one half from the larger incomes. A man with £100,000 a year will grumble badly if you cut him down to £50,000, but he can carry on on £50,000. The £200 a year man cannot carry on on £100 a year.

We may lay it down, then, as a general principle that high taxation can be levied with more success in proportion as

---

* We enjoy in this country, for instance, the power of raising for Revenue near double the amount obtainable from a rival population of much the same size and much the same wealth, but one in which more than half that population are economically free.

property is ill-distributed: high taxation is incompatible with a wide and equitable distribution of ownership.

But what interests us most is the converse proposition – that high taxation being hostile to well distributed property is, in its very essence, hostile to every attempt, such as is ours, to begin a restoration of property. Introduce high taxation into society where well distributed property exists, and you cannot levy it with ease; insofar as you do levy it, you will begin to impair the good distribution of property in that society, but there is every chance that you will fail. Attempt, however, to cultivate the beginnings of property in a society when high taxation is already permanent and you will find that effort wasted, unless the rules of taxation are drastically modified. That is the main quarrel which those who desire to reconstruct property (if that be possible), in our modern diseased capitalist state, must have with the present enormity of taxation; that is why they must regard it as mortal to their effort. If it is continued on existing lines, the new effort at recreating small property cannot thrive.

The reason for this should be obvious when we consider by what process property is gradually brought into existence amid a proletarian society. It is brought into existence by gradual accumulation; by thrift; by adding to building, to the value of land occupied, to liquid capital in hand, to investments. To recreate small property in society under the curse of Industrial Capitalism requires many other conditions; it requires security, it requires a sound currency, based on some real material, preferably gold or silver, or both. It requires one not to be tampered with by Government or "managers." It requires special favour for the small man at the expense of the large one, special laws interfering with undue accumulation – and so on. But it also demands moderation in taxation. Under a Capitalist régime, where everything depends upon keeping a margin of profit between the proletarian earnings and the total amount of production, and therefore the leaving of mere wages as little taxed as possible, taxation must be thrown as much as possible on to property. It begins to put a brake upon the accumulation of small property the moment that accumulation arises.

The small man is thinking of building on to his premises with his savings, but the rates are 15 shillings in the pound, and he pauses. The small man has accumulated investments which bring him in so much a year; he knows that if he passes a certain limit the increasing steepness of the tax he has to pay will become burdensome. The professional man is earning an income out of which he can build up property for the future by saving, say, a third of his income. But if he is so successful or works so hard that he reaches the point where a full quarter of his income is taken away in taxation, it is hardly worth his while to save more, and he will cease to save.

It is true that high taxation does not produce its worst effects in the very beginnings of small property, it comes to have such effects rather when the accumulation is of a certain respectable size, and is beginning to attach to what we call "the Middle Class Standard." But then *to preserve and to create the Middle Class Standard is of the very first importance to the creation and preservation of property in the State.*

This is perhaps the most important point in the whole of this discussion, not only as regards the effect of taxation, but in every other department. It cannot be too much repeated and insisted upon that the ideal of property does not comport equality in property – that mechanical ideal is contradictory of the personal quality attaching to property. It is not a bad but a good thing that rents, the dwelling house, the income from investment, and the rest, should be upon various scales, for such variety corresponds to the complex reality of human society. What *is* a bad thing is that the destitute wage slaves – a proletariat – should form the determining member of society, and that real production and thrift and personal effort – in other words, work and citizenship – should be encouraged. Under a system of high taxation the gambler escapes while the same taxation kills the man who is trying to save.

Consider the two types of man in our society whom anyone of us can observe in action. The one works steadily at, let us say, some small distributing business, a shop; his ideal is to prosper within the limits of the middle class. He will rise perhaps from profits of two or three hundred a year to profits of four, five, six hundred a year; he will lay by money for investment; he will die possessed of a house worth, say, £2,000, and will at last be receiving an income from his business and his savings of, say, £1,000 a year. Such a man under a system of low taxation progresses uniformly and reaps a reward not unconnected with his industry and intelligence. The same is true of a man who makes similar progress through application to a profession. Apply high taxation after a certain point to either of these and the process ceases. It is not worth the worker's while to make the extra effort.*

Now consider the other type, the man who speculates, who gambles, whose ideal is not a solid middle class ending to his efforts, but a larger fortune or ruin. See how he goes to work.

He risks the complete loss of his first accumulation, and more often than not suffers that complete loss. If (commonly through no good judgement of his own, but by blind accident) the gamble comes off, he is suddenly heavily enriched; and nine times out of ten the form of the enrichment is such that the fisc has no hold upon it. His gains are advantitious, and not taxed as part of a regular income.

He gambles again – again he either ruins himself (as more commonly happens) or again pulls it off. And that second gamble makes him already a conspicuously rich man. He

---

* Mr. H.G. Wells has put the point with his customary lucidity. He said (in effect): "Suppose a man to be making, say by writing, X£s a year on which the taxation is ¼. He has a real income of $(3X/4)=(27X/36X)$. Let him by extra drudgery add a third to his old nominal income, that is an extra $X/3$. He has now a total taxable income of $48X/36$. But on this higher income the veto is no longer ¼ but ⅓. He has a real income of $32X/36$. He has added to his real income by $5X/36$, but he has had to earn another $12X/36$ to get that increment. *More than half* of his extra effort has been thrown away. He is taxed on that extra effort, not ⅓ but more than ½."

can then, as our industrial society is organized, advance with more certitude and less risk, to a fortune, five, ten or ninety times greater than that which had already put him among the wealthy.

When he is upon that scale high taxation begins to operate upon him forcibly; he has an income which is almost wholly assessable, and, in spite of the various forms of evasion, his huge accumulation will more often than not fall under the full operation of the Death Duties. But he remains very rich.

All through his career – which has done nothing but harm to the Commonwealth – and to his own character – a career destructive of citizenship in himself and in others – the fisc has been positively encouraging him to take his choice between ruin, perhaps imprisonment, and a great fortune. All through the career of the opposite type, the fisc has been putting the brake on the accumulation of moderate property. In other words, high taxation destroys the middle class. It dries up the stream by which a middle class is brought into existence and maintained. It breeds plutocracy.

The process is aggravated in the modern world from the fact that very great fortunes alone today are fairly secure. The more the disease of Industrial Capitalism develops the higher the point below which the investor is uncertain of the future. Therefore men who might not otherwise be tempted to gamble are urged to gamble, and those whose instincts are for slow progressive accumulation are discouraged.

There is another aspect of this evil, this destruction of the Middle Class by high taxation; and that is that the middle class being the spokesman for property, property lies undefended when a middle class fails. Through a middle class property, as an institution, becomes vocal because it can express itself upon a basis of leisure and cultivation; it has inevitably been found in the past that when the middle class weakens or is destroyed, even though there remain widespread property in the hands of quite small men, these are at the mercy of the very great fortunes which stand above them, with no intermediary layer. For the very wealthy control society. That is exactly what happened in the breakdown of the ancient pagan civilization and, where Capitalism is at its worst, it is what we see happening today.

But when we have determined that high taxation is mortal to well distributed property, and especially to the proper functioning of that "flywheel," which we call the Middle Class, we are still left with the fact that high taxation is present and must be faced.

It has come upon the modern world as the result of two causes; the waging of war upon an unprecedented scale financed by Bank Credit at interest, instead of by a levy upon capital, and the increase of State Socialism for the purpose of guaranteeing Capitalism against a revolt of the proletariat. The first is called "interest on War Loans" or "a National Debt," the second is called "Social Services."

It would seem that both these categories of public expenditure are inevitable as things now stand, and that, therefore, this prime obstacle to our effort – high taxation – will remain and will make our effort futile, at least in those countries where the mass of the people are already proletarian, that is, in those countries which are generally industrialized – and of these, of course, Great Britain is the chief example. Our society, here in England, is that one society among the great nations in which the people have been most thoroughly dispossessed. It is also – and on that account – the society in which the very highest taxation can be levied with the least friction.

And how, things being what they are, can such a situation be met? If we cut down beyond a certain limit the so-called "social services," the Capitalist machine will break down through the revolt or (more probably) the increasing lethargy of its proletariat. If we cut down beyond a certain limit the interest paid upon public debt, State credit will be impaired or destroyed. In other words, we seem to have come to a situation in which extravagantly high taxation is necessarily permanent. Is there any way out of this situation?

There is evidently the catastrophic way; already in the last 14 years catastrophic steps one after the other have reduced a burden which otherwise could not have been borne at all. The German Reich has destroyed the whole of its public debt by repudiation; the French have destroyed four-fifths of theirs; the Italians two-thirds; and we in this country by a mixture of repudiation, what was virtually forced conversion, and the debasing of the currency (issuing of bad money), have reduced the burden by over half. Yet what remains is sufficiently grievous, in Great Britain at least, to militate against the reconstruction of property in our midst.

Will further castastrophic steps relieve us to the point where individual thrift and work will come into play again for the creation of reasonable private accumulations? It is probable: it is not certain. What is certain is that if the level of high taxation continues we shall end with a state of society wherein there will stand contrasted a few very great fortunes on one side and a proletarian mass upon the other, with all hope for the reconstrution of property abandoned.

VII

HERE REMAIN TO BE CONSIDERED THREE POINTS. How those who aim at the reconstruction of property should deal with large scale distribution; how they should proceed in order to maintain the life of the first experiments; and, in direct connection with this last, how they should deal with the function of credit.

1. As to large distribution: wholesale exchange (the merchant as contrasted with the shopkeeper) has become "Big Business," working on another scale and in a different fashion from retail exchange.

Retail exchange has its department stores and chain shops, but it also presents to this day a very great number of small domestic concerns. There is no positive law as yet to prevent the small man attempting to start his individual shop, and though he is heavily handicapped as against the large shop or the chain of shops, he may struggle on. But wholesale exchange and all the machinery of it have been captured by highly centralized capitalism. A handful of men control, and control in permanent fashion (for example) the sending of jute to England. A comparatively small body of men control the reception of wheat in bulk by this country: and so with all the main articles of our import. So also with the handling of the wholesale internal exchanges. There remain, of course, a very large number of small wholesale men engaged in distribution of various kinds, but the markets, as a whole, are dominated by a few, and increasingly so.

Now the rule to remember in this department of our effort is that insisted upon through this essay: we are not attempting a universal and immediate revolution and it would be absurd to do so. The Communists have only to follow on the lines of existing capitalism, which has given them birth and in spiritual sympathy with which they work in every practical detail of their programme. Those who, in a much more successful and immediate fashion, are setting up the Servile State, start entirely from Capitalism and are developing of their nature on capitalistic lines. The only economic difference between a herd of subservient Russians and a mob of free Englishmen pouring into a factory of a morning, is that the latter are exploited for private profit, the former by the State in communal fashion. The motive of the Russian masters is to establish a comfortable bureaucracy for themselves and their friends out of proletarian labour. But *we* want something different from either.

We are attempting a radical change. We are attempting a reactionary revolution: perhaps impossible. Thus even where we have to accept centralized power we shall try to get the profits payable severally to very many citizens, and we shall try to make small industry preferred in the use of that power and to prevent its being centralized for the advantage of large units.

Now, as we are attempting to reverse an almost irresistible current which is now long established and has dug its bed deep, we can only attempt small beginnings. To change to a metaphor which I have already used, as we are trying to reafforest a vast area which has gone back to desert through the cutting down of trees, we can only begin by replanting carefully and section by section, artificially protecting our tender seedlings until we have established some few areas whence trees can spread.

Therefore we cannot attack in a frontal manner nor all along the line the established domination of large capital in wholesale exchange. Our chance is to begin with retail exchange and build up from that.

All we can do in the matter of wholesale exchange until we are strong enough to affect the mass of it, is to guard the small man jealously from discrimination by the wholesale provider. Still more must we safeguard him against being turned into a mere servant of the wholesale provider. The function of so guarding him we must leave not only to special laws in his favour, but to the bye-laws of his Guild as I shall presently propose.

2. The safeguarding of the small unit, the seedlings of reafforestation, the delicate experiments in the reconstruction of property, must take the form of the Guild: not the unprotected guild arising spontaneously (for that would soon be killed by the predatory capitalism around it) but of the Guild *chartered and established by positive law.*

Now the Guild, which is the essential institution for safeguarding small capital, should be established particularly in the case of crafts, next in the case of retail trade, and only in the third place in the case of the wage earner, the destitute man, the existing slave of capitalism.

This is, of course, to reverse altogether the existing order of development in which the wage earners trades unions comes first in strength, the craft union a bad second, and the mutual support of small retail traders is weakest of all. But this state of affairs arose out of capitalism, whereas we are fighting capitalism, and therefore we must begin with the craft guild and the shop guild.

Such guilds *might* be formed on a small scale to begin with. The natural instinct of men still retaining political freedom though they have lost economic freedom is to form associations in defence. When the common morals of Europe were thrown to the winds in the religious chaos of the Reformation, the organs of economic self-defence were destroyed. The only two guilds that survive today in England are those of the lawyers and the doctors. But the instinct for self-preservation was so strong that even the unfortunate wage slaves began to combine in defence of a standard wage. It is one of the glories of the English that in spite of the most cruel persecution, they managed in a confused way to build up amid wage slavery certain organizations which were a distant echo of the old guild system of their free ancestors. Proletarian England produced the trades unions, some few of which became really effective for the partial protection of a minority of the population.

There was, however, no attempt to act thus for the safeguarding of property. The organized village community went under. The small shopkeeper in part, the small craftsman almost wholly, went under. The dykes protecting small property from the ravages of competition were thoroughly broken down.

Now it is our business to build them up again today. We cannot, of course, attempt to do so on a large scale. We might create a guild of this or that particular craft: for instance, of cabinet makers. We might create a guild of this or that particular retail trade: for instance, publicans or tobacconists, or of private makers and menders and sellers of footwear. We might propose, and with the right political machinery carry out, charters whereby the Guild should be established with due limits, should admit to practice certain trades, supervise good work therein, prevent the growth of one unit at the expense of the average small craftsman or small shopkeeper – and so on. But we would at first only do very little. Our hope must be that such experiments on a small scale will give the example and spread. Our hope cannot yet be that this example will give, save in a long space of time, its note to the community.

But here comes in a very important question. Can the political machinery whereby this reform, or indeed, any wholesome human reform could come about, be framed in a community whereof the laws are, in theory at least, framed by parliaments?

Parliaments are necessarily the organs of plutocracy. There is no approach through them whereby the small man can have effect in the economic field. No approach to the guild system, even as a modest and partial experiment, can be expected until political power is decentralized and rearranged according to economic classes and interests. As the parliamentary system decays (and it is going to pieces very rapidly throughout Europe) monarchy or some unexpected revival of public opinion might impose the restitution of charters. Parliaments as we have them now will certainly not do so. Money and the limelight are the motive forces directing parliamentarians. There is neither money nor limelight in the guild idea to attract any parliamentarian towards it.

With the re-establishment of the guilds comes the question of chartering (that is, of establishing with legal safeguards) the proletarians' trades unions.

That is certainly no part of our ideal, for the trades union only came into existence as a function of wage slavery. It is a proletarian institution through and through, and a proletariat and proletarian spirit is exactly what we are aiming to destroy. But on the way to the proprietary state chartering of trades unions would give a good example. Some of our greater unions today, though not officially chartered, have in practice attained many of the powers which an official charter would give. They, in practice, regulate wages, consider the opportunities of employment, prevent their function from being swamped with numbers, and in general substitute status and order for chaotic competition.

It would be possible to begin by regularizing these few successful experiments, by giving them a legal basis, and using them as models for extension into other fields. At any rate the idea of the guild is the idea that must inspire all our efforts to re-establish economic security combined with economic freedom. Even if we only did it in very small beginnings, we could soon recognize the tests of success. If people could not obtain properly made craftsman furniture, save from a man admitted to the Guild and subject to its rules, we should know that in that one small department we had achieved success. Again, the first man fined or sent to prison for trying to establish under false names a chain of retail shops would be a test of success. The first working of an appeal to the Guild against the bad workmanship of a craftsman, or against the coercion of a small distributor by a wholesale provider, would be a test of success. Even though the thing were exceptional and applying at first only to a very few categories of small production and exchange, it could be planted and might strike root.

3. Dealing with the function of credit is not fundamental to the restoration and maintenance of property. Credit is not a vital element in all societies; it is not a permanent and general social, economic or political problem. The modern function of credit is of comparatively recent development; it has already gone woefully wrong, and appears to be approaching catastrophe. Credit, then, is only a local and ephemeral issue. Nevertheless, it must be dealt with, because for the moment it monstrously overshadows our civic life.

On its largest lines the function of credit (in this modern sense) is as follows:—

The means of production and exchange and the very currency itself can only be set in motion through the banks. In a modern highly industrialized community, and in England above all, the banks form a monopoly, which decides what machinery shall be set in motion for the production of what wealth, in what amount and by whom. Into the hands of these institutions of credit are placed in larger and larger proportions the natural forces and the stores of goods without which nothing can be made; and at the discretion of the banks is purchasing power doled out.

The organization of this system as at present developed after only a few generations and more particularly in the last hundred years, has become in highly industrialized countries, and especially in England, both universal and all-powerful. All payments of significant amount are now made in this country by cheque and nearly all initiative depends upon the support of the banking monopoly which issues, or refuses to issue, a promise to honour cheques. The bank credit at work, being ten times the actual deposits, holds the throttle valve of the whole economic machine. It is of no use attempting to restore the institution of property here in England now until we have given the small owner some power of reaction against this universal master.

Now in this problem, as in every other problem of our enquiry, the main rules remain the same. We cannot make a frontal attack, nor can we attempt a universal and immediate change. We can only work piecemeal and from humble beginnings.

We can, indeed, on the negative side support the very useful work that is being done by many others who do not sympathize with our ideals. We can spread, (and it is the duty of every good citizen to spread), a knowledge of the arbitrary power possessed by modern banks, and proclaim the duty of controlling it. *That* general action is open to us, and of great service it is. But we cannot rapidly produce a well divided control of credit nor attack on any ready-made plan the gigantic network of credit control which has arisen almost within living memory and half strangles society. What we can do is to establish small co-operative credit institutions duly chartered and legally protected from attack.

Meanwhile any development of the guild system would modify the position of the banks and weaken their monopoly.

As small property gradually developed, the banking monopoly would progressively lose more and more of its power. For instance, bank credit, by law of its being, discriminates in favour of the big capitalist and against the small man; but it would begin to sing a different tune when it had to meet the power of organized corporations of small men, and when differential taxation began to make it more and more difficult for the large unit, no matter how well supported by bank credit, to eat up the small.

It is not practical to suggest a public control of the banking monopoly from above, by the central power of government, save in the case of the national central banks. These being national functions should, quite obviously, be responsible to whatever speaks and acts for the nation. Being the most highly centralized of all social functions, they should be directly at the orders of the central power. But for the rest of the established banking system, it cannot be displaced. Its activities can only be modified by the gradual growth of well distributed ownership.

Meanwhile there should be fostered the spread, side by side with the present banking monopoly, of these properly chartered co-operative banks, connected with the guilds of every description. Such popular institutions of credit could not subsist for a moment against the hostility of the independent banking monopoly (which is today more powerful than the State) unless they were supported by privilege: positive laws protecting them and charters of their own. But granted such charters and laws safeguarding them from assault and murder, popular co-operative banks might increase in function. They might even end – just possibly, though most improbably – by transforming the credit system as a whole, and making it the subject of those small units which build up the guild.

* * * *

WITH THIS, I end what are but a series of short suggestions upon the method by which a reaction against Capitalism and its product, Communism, may be begun. These suggestions are few and obviously imperfect. Others will add to and perfect them. But the main task remains: not that of elaborating machinery for the reaction towards right living, but of forwarding the spirit of that reaction in a society which has almost forgotten what property and its concomitant freedom means.

Notes

1. The Douglas Scheme. A reference to the "Social Credit" monetary theory and practical scheme formulated by Major C.H. Douglas (1879– 1952), as expressed in his work by the same name (1924), as well as his other works, including *Economic Democracy* (1920), *The Monopoly of Credit* (1931), *The Use of Money* (1935). The system advocated a National Dividend being distributed to all citizens, in order to aid in the stabilization of prices, the restoration of purchasing power, and the reform of the evils of debt-based money and fractional reserve banking. Once implemented, the scheme was supposed to lead to the creation of the Leisure State.

2. Alfred Richard Orage (1873–1934). English social thinker and journalist, who was one of the main exponents of the doctrine of the National Guilds. He became joint editor in 1907 of *The New Age*, of which from 1909 until 1922 he was the sole editor and dominant spirit. Some years after he resigned from editorship of that journal, Orage began editing another one, the *New English Weekly*, which he continued to do until his death in 1934.

3. Tigris and Euphrates. The two rivers which supplied water for the irrigation of the farmland between them and thus supported the great civilizations of Mesopotamia. The Tigris, some 1,840 km long, has its origins in southeast Turkey but is largely supplied by tributaries in Iraq. The Euphrates begins in the highlands of eastern Turkey and exits in the Persian Gulf; it is roughly 2,700km in length. The rivers join at Qurna in Iraq. Belloc's comment on the action of the Mongols is a reference to their destruction of Iraq in 1258.

4. Fabian. A member of the Fabian Society. This organization was founded in 1884 to bring about a Socialist State, not through armed insurrection or violence, but by incremental politics, piecemeal legislation and peer group pressure.

5. John Stuart Mill (1806–1873). English philosopher and political economist. Mill was extraordinarily intelligent; he learned Greek by the age of 3. He is remembered chiefly as an advocate of "utilitarianism," a philosophy of

ethics which maintains, in opposition to the classical and Catholic notion of virtue, that an action is good or bad based upon its social consequences. Despite this essential scepticism, his *Principles of Political Economy* (1848) was regarded as a thorough and methodical treatment of economics; it has been regarded both as an apologetic for Capitalism, in the *lassiez-faire* tradition, and a treatise supporting Socialism (because of Mill's belief that an ideal economy would be based on worker-owned co-operatives).

6. Elizabeth I (1533–1603). Elizabeth Tudor, Queen of England from 1558 to 1603, daughter of Henry VIII who declared himself Supreme Head of the Church in England as a result of Rome's refusal to grant an annulment of his marriage to Catherine. She was no friend of Catholicism; nonetheless, Belloc could say of her, in his *Elizabethan Commentary*: "We must remember her isolation, her lack of anything that could support her soul, her lack even of what people in her position have a right to demand, the security of the future."

7. William Morris (1834–1896). English artist, author, journalist, and social activist. A chief Victorian-era critic of Industrialism, he was an eclectic Socialist who was also variously influenced by the High Anglican "Oxford Movement" of Newman, Keble and Pusey, and the legacy of medieval life and art. In 1856, he embarked on an artistic career, becoming famous for his poetry, his wallpapers, his designs, his writings and his typography; he became the chief inspiration behind the Arts and Crafts movement (1870-1900) which desired to elevate the applied arts to the status of fine arts, and to restore a human scale and dimension to production of useful goods. His critique of Industrialism led him to embrace Socialism; in 1884 he founded the Socialist League, and for a time was editor of its journal, *Commonweal*.

8. Bilbao and Leon. Cities in northern Spain about 200 km apart. Bilbao is situated in the Basque region of Northern Spain, facing the Bay of Biscay; Leon is about 150km due South of the center of the northern coastline.

9. Charles II (1630–1685). King of England from 1660 to 1685. Fought in the Civil War against the Puritans, which ended with the execution of his father, Charles I, in 1649. He returned to England following the dissolution of the Cromwellian Commonwealth, and converted to Catholicism on his deathbed. In *Charles II: The Last Rally*, Belloc characterizes Charles's reign as largely "a struggle between Monarchy and Money-Power."

10. William Cobbett (1763–1835). Writer, farmer, ruralist, and political journalist. He was born to poor parents in Hampshire in England, and rose to become one of the most famous polemical journalists of his day. His reputation was based on his fearlessness and his profound integrity; he spent most of his energy attacking corruption in government. He wrote 17 major works, and in 1802 he founded the *Political Register*, which he managed until his death. At a time when Catholics were still being persecuted

About IHS Press

IHS Press believes that the key to the restoration of Catholic Society is the recovery and the implementation of the wisdom our Fathers in the Faith possessed so fully less than a century ago. At a time when numerous ideologies were competing for supremacy, these men articulated, with precision and vigor, and without apology or compromise, the only genuine alternative to the then- (and still-) prevailing currents of thought: value-free and yet bureaucratic "progressivism" on the one hand, and the rehashed, *laissez-faire* free-for-all of "conservatism" on the other. That alternative is the Social Teaching of the Catholic Church.

Catholic Social Teaching offers the solutions to the political, economic, and social problems that plague modern society; problems that stem from the false principles of the Reformation, Renaissance, and Revolution, and which are exacerbated by the secularization and industrialization of society that has since continued. Defending, explaining, and applying this Teaching was the business of the great Social Catholics of last century. Unfortunately, much of their work is today both unknown and unavailable.

Thus, IHS Press was founded in September of 2001 A.D. as the only publisher dedicated exclusively to the Social Teaching of the Church, helping Catholics of the third millennium pick up where those of last century left off. IHS Press is committed to recovering, and helping others to rediscover, the valuable works of the Catholic economists, historians, and social critics. To that end, IHS Press is in the business of issuing critical editions of works on society, politics, and economics by writers, thinkers, and men of action such as Hilaire Belloc, Gilbert Chesterton, Arthur Penty, Fr. Vincent McNabb, Fr. Denis Fahey, Jean Ousset, Amintore Fanfani, George O'Brien, and others, making the wisdom they contain available to the current generation.

It is the aim of IHS Press to issue these vitally important works in high-quality volumes and at reasonable prices, to enable the widest possible audience to acquire, enjoy, and benefit from them. Such an undertaking cannot be maintained without the support of generous benefactors. With that in mind, IHS Press was constituted as a not-for-profit corporation which is exempt from federal tax according to Section 501(c)(3) of the United States Internal Revenue Code. Donations to IHS Press are, therefore, tax deductible, and are especially welcome to support its continued operation, and to help it with the publication of new titles and the more widespread dissemination of those already in print.

For more information, contact us at:

mail: 222 W. 21st St., Suite F-122~Norfolk, VA 23517 USA
toll-free telephone or fax: 877-IHS-PRES (877.447.7737)
e-mail: order@ihspress.com • *internet:* www.ihspress.com

IHS Press is a tax-exempt 501(c)(3) corporation; EIN: 54-2057581.
Applicable documentation is available upon request.

in England, he found the courage to write that "the Protestant religion had been established by gibbets, racks and ripping knives," though Cobbett himself was not Catholic.

11. Wyndham Land Purchase Act. Introduced in the British Parliament in 1903 by George Wyndham (1863–1913), and which sought to give tenant farmers in Ireland the right to buy the property that they farmed and encouraged such purchase by offering incentives to landlords who sold. The Act was a response to the growing Land Agitation amongst the Irish who had been dispossessed by the English governing class in preceding centuries.